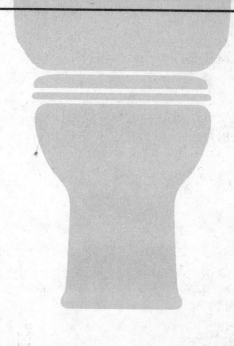

ARE YOU
SH*TTING ME?

ARE YOU
SH*TTING ME?

1,004 FACTS

THAT WILL SCARE THE
SH*T OUT OF YOU

CARY McNEAL

A PERIGEE BOOK

A PERIGEE BOOK
Published by the Penguin Group
Penguin Group (USA) LLC
375 Hudson Street, New York, New York 10014

USA • Canada • UK • Ireland • Australia • New Zealand • India • South Africa • China

penguin.com

A Penguin Random House Company

ARE YOU SH*TTING ME?

ISBN: 978-0-399-16819-2

An application to register this book for cataloging has been submitted to the Library of Congress.

First edition: October 2014

PRINTED IN THE UNITED STATES OF AMERICA

10   9   8   7   6   5

Text design by Pauline Neuwirth

While the author has made every effort to provide accurate telephone numbers, Internet addresses, and other contact information at the time of publication, neither the publisher nor the author assumes any responsibility for errors, or for changes that occur after publication. Further, the publisher does not have any control over and does not assume any responsibility for author or third-party websites or their content.

Most Perigee books are available at special quantity discounts for bulk purchases for sales promotions, premiums, fund-raising, or educational use. Special books, or book excerpts, can also be created to fit specific needs. For details, write: Special.Markets@us.penguingroup.com.

CONTENTS

INTRODUCTION

WELCOME TO MY BOOK. I hope you enjoy it. What's to enjoy about being frightened, you ask? That's a good question. I suppose it's like watching a horror movie: you know it's going to freak you out, but you buy the ticket—or, in this case, the book—anyway. Maybe you like the thrill of fear. Maybe you're a glutton for punishment. Or maybe someone gave the book to you as a gift. They might think you don't have enough fiber in your diet.

What about me? Do I write these books because I'm a sadist? Nah. When it comes to scary business, I believe that forewarned is forearmed. Think of me as someone who's trying to help you by educating you. Because I'm a nice guy like that.

If you want to learn more about any topic herein, check out the source list at the back of the book for links to more information. If you've read the other two books in this series, *1,000 Facts That Will Scare the Sh*t Out of You* and *Scared Sh*tless*, welcome back and thanks for your support.

For the rest of you: Be afraid.

CM

1

Florida

WHAT'S SCARY ABOUT FLORIDA, you ask? Besides the fact that it looks like a giant wiener? I could cite any number of things: Casey Anthony, George Zimmerman, hanging chads, alligators, Key West, Lynyrd Skynyrd. Instead, I will ask you, which state do you think of whenever you hear a news story about someone eating someone else's face off or a guy shooting up a Burger King with a bazooka because they didn't hold the pickles on his Whopper Jr.? Right:

Florida. And if you don't think of Florida first, you're not paying attention.

FACT 1 **A mother–daughter duo in Tampa are partners in pornography.** Jessica and Monica Sexxxton post home movies on their own site and will have sex with the same person at the same time, though they claim they never touch each other on camera. Whew! For a minute there I was creeped out.

- -

FACT 2 In 2012, fifty-year-old cougar Jennie Scott of Manatee County was arrested for beating the crap out of her thirty-two-year-old boyfriend after **he climaxed first during a 69 love-session** and refused to continue pleasuring her.

- -

FACT 3 A Jacksonville man, Allen Casey, was arrested in 2012 for hitting his boyfriend in the face with a plate for playing too much Alanis Morissette music. Casey defended himself to police, saying, **"That's all that motherfucker listens to."**

FACT 4 👉 In July 2013, Josue Rodriguez of Lake Worth **attacked his roommate with a machete** after the roommate changed the radio station while Rodriguez was in the shower. Who keeps a machete in the shower?

- -

FACT 5 👉 **Three San Mateo men were arrested in 2013 for stealing a nine-foot-tall, six-hundred-pound purple aluminum chicken from a roadside stand.**

- -

FACT 6 👉 A Lake County man was arrested in June 2013 for leaving **nude photos of his former roommate** on the cars of the roommate's co-workers and grandmother after the roommate moved out. The victim had allowed the photos to be taken in return for room and board.

- -

FACT 7 👉 Kingsley Lake, or "Silver Dollar Lake," is **almost a perfect circle**, spanning nearly two thousand acres with a surprising depth of ninety feet. The reason for the popular lake's unique shape and depth? It is one of Florida's many sinkholes.

FACT 8 👉 In August 2013, 150 law enforcement officers in full riot gear were called to Avon Park Youth Academy, an all-male juvenile correctional facility, when rioting inmates **set fire to parts of the building** and caused hundreds of thousands of dollars' worth of damage. The riot broke out after the losers of a basketball game refused to make good on their original wager: three containers of Cup Noodles.

FACT 9 👉 According to the *New York Post*, most of the seven hundred rhesus monkeys captured in recent years around Silver Springs, Florida, **tested positive for the herpes B virus**.

FACT 10 👉 Miami suffers from an **infestation of giant African land snails**, which can grow to the size of rats. The snails consume plants, stucco, and plaster, and can cause significant structural damage to homes and businesses.

FACT 11 👉 **Giant African land snails were likely introduced to Florida by a practitioner of Santería**, a religion that uses the creatures in rituals.

are you sh*tting me?

FACT 12 👉 Some giant African land snails carry a **parasitic lungworm** that, if transmitted to humans, can cause illnesses including meningitis.

FACT 13 👉 Florida is infested with an estimated **150,000 nonnative Burmese pythons**. Often pets that have been released into the wild, the twelve- to thirteen-foot creatures have disrupted the food chain in the Everglades.

FACT 14 👉 The Florida Fish and Wildlife Conservation Commission has created a **tournament to kill invasive Burmese pythons** in the Everglades, offering cash prizes to hunters who destroy the most and the largest snakes.

FACT 15 👉 The rock or North African python is also establishing a population east of the Everglades. More aggressive than Burmese pythons, **rock pythons are responsible for the deaths of two Canadian children** and a sixty-pound family dog in West Kendall.

FACT 16 🖙 Florida game officials fear that the growing populations of rock and Burmese pythons will mate and **create a "super snake."** Both animals are in the top five largest species of snakes in the world.

FACT 17 🖙 In November 2013, a sixth grader at a Collier County middle school was suspended for **setting off the fire alarm by twerking into it**. The student was suspended because the school had been declared a "Twerk-Free Zone."

FACT 18 🖙 An Ocala man was arrested in November 2013 for reportedly **terrorizing and chasing an eight-year-old** after the child refused to share his potato chips.

FACT 19 🖙 An Allapattah man was busted in December 2013 after he caught **a four-foot-long alligator** and tried to barter it for a twelve-pack of beer at a convenience store.

FACT 20 🖙 In a March 2013 attempt to keep her local beach clean, a Stock Island woman confronted and **brawled with a littering spring breaker, biting her in the cheek**.

FACT 21 ☞ Residents of a Tampa apartment complex captured a twelve-foot alligator from a river in October 2013 and **leashed it to a tree to keep as a pet**. Other residents told law enforcement that people "had caught [the alligator] and was feeding it cats." The animal was ultimately removed by authorities and destroyed.

FACT 22 ☞ A Duval County high school is being asked via a petition on Change.org to change its name. The school, the student body of which is predominantly black, is named after Nathan Bedford Forrest, a Confederate Army general and the **first grand wizard of the Ku Klux Klan**.

FACT 23 ☞ Convicted murderers Robert Mackey and Paul Trucchio of Volusia County were said to have **prayed to "the alligator god"**— in this case a concrete statue—in hopes that the wild animals would eat the body of their victim, Lorraine Hatzakorzian.

FACT 24 ☞ Hatzakorzian's severed head was found in the Everglades, but **the rest of her body remains missing**.

FACT 25 👉 A Bradenton man was arrested on misdemeanor battery charges in January 2013 for **giving unsuspecting strangers wedgies**.

FACT 26 👉 In October 2013, an Escambia County man was arrested on felony child abuse charges for reportedly **beating his daughter to the tune of Robin Thicke's "Blurred Lines."** Someone should beat Robin Thicke to the tune of Robin Thicke's "Blurred Lines."

FACT 27 👉 When a Palm Bay man got into an argument with his girlfriend in January 2013 while dropping her off at work at Taco Bell, **he bit off her thumb**. Doctors were unable to save the severed digit.

FACT 28 👉 An Orlando man was arrested in November 2013 for attacking his pregnant sister by **grabbing her neck and throwing her into a nightstand** after she ate his chicken nuggets.

 are you sh*tting me?

FACT 29    In November 2013, a Gibsonton woman renewed her wedding vows with her "husband"— a Ferris wheel she named Bruce. **She wanted a mate who would stay around.** *rim shot*

FACT 30   A Pensacola woman stopped traffic in August 2013 when she stood on the roadside asking for breast implant donations by carrying a sign that read, **"Not Homeless, Need Boobs."**

FACT 31   In October 2013, a grieving Sarasota man was questioned after **sprinkling the ashes of his deceased fiancée in LensCrafters** of the Westfield Southgate Mall. The man said that he was spreading the ashes in places that had been special to the dead woman. She must have really loved their one-hour lens guarantee.

2

Ancient Medical Practices

YOU KNOW WHAT WAS great about going to the doctor in centuries past? Nothing, that's what. Not a damn thing. That is, unless you like the idea of having a hole drilled in your head or leeches clamped on your nipples or gallons of blood drained from your body every time you dared complain of a headache.

No, wait, there was one good thing back then: you didn't have to wait an hour to see the doctor. Why? Because you were the only idiot there.

FACT 32 👉 **The use of maggots to clean wounds** has proven to be effective for patients who don't respond to traditional treatments. Or who have difficulty vomiting.

FACT 33 👉 The arrival of antibiotics in the twentieth century made the use of maggots fall out of favor, but the method is now making a comeback and is used today in some hospitals to treat conditions like **leg ulcers, pressure sores, and infected surgical wounds**.

FACT 34 👉 **Hairballs save lives**—or at least they saved some lives in the 1600s, when aristocrats were often the targets of assassination attempts by arsenic poisoning. Bezoars, or hairballs from goats and sheep, were placed in drinks to absorb any arsenic that might have been put there. The drinks were horrible, but at least drinkers didn't die.

FACT 35 👉 Modern research has proven how the ancient method was effective: **sulfur compounds** in the hair proteins of a bezoar bind to the toxic agents in arsenic, rendering them harmless.

FACT 36 👉 **Trepanation**, the medical practice of cutting into the skull, dates back to the Stone Age. Ancient Egyptians believed that trepanation could help alleviate pressure on the brain, while physicians in the Middle Ages thought the practice would release evil spirits from the possessed.

FACT 37 👉 Trepanation is **still used in some countries today** to treat ailments ranging from fatigue to epilepsy to depression. You're still depressed after the procedure, but at least you know why: you have a gaping hole in your head.

FACT 38 👉 Sixteenth-century women would **apply puppy urine to their faces**, believing it was beneficial to the skin's health and complexion. I'm wondering if they collected the urine first or just held puppies over their heads.

FACT 39 👉   The ancient medical practice of **bloodletting** involves draining blood from the body to help cure disease. Believed to have originated in ancient Egypt, the practice was the main therapy used by doctors for thousands of years.

FACT 40 👉   In the Middle Ages, bloodletting was **often performed by barbers**, which is why the traditional barber's pole—like the bloody towels that once hung outside barber shops—is colored red and white.

FACT 41 👉   After a twelfth-century church edict prohibited monks and priests from performing bloodletting, barbers added the procedure to their list of offered services, along with **cupping, tooth extractions, lancing, and even amputations**.

FACT 42 👉   To determine a patient's health, a barber surgeon would study the color of the patient's urine, and sometimes **smell and even taste it**—yes, taste it.

are you sh*tting me?

FACT 43 👉 Patients frequently died during treatment by bloodletting. **George Washington died after giving five to seven pints of blood** in twenty-four hours to cure a throat infection.

FACT 44 👉 Ancient Egyptian physicians believed that **leech therapy could cure symptoms** for a variety of illnesses, from fevers to flatulence.

FACT 45 👉 In the 1800s, **women had leeches placed in their vaginas** to treat conditions like vaginal discharge and cervical cancer.

FACT 46 👉 Leeches were applied to the clitoris to **treat nymphomania** and other female complaints.

FACT 47 👉 Leeches still have medical applications today, as their saliva has been found to **promote circulation and speed the healing of damaged tissue**.

FACT 48  The leech is invaluable to surgeons who are faced with the difficulties of **reattaching minute veins**, which clot easily, in procedures such as limb and scalp reattachments, limb transplants, skin flap surgery, and breast reconstruction.

FACT 49 The ancient Greek doctor Galen recommended **the use of electric eels** for treating headaches and facial pain.

FACT 50 Eels were also used by the ancient Greeks and Romans **to treat gout**; the patient would stand on an eel until his foot became numb. This paved the way for today's popular Dr. Scholl's Eel Inserts.

FACT 51 One American doctor in the early 1900s **treated mental illness by removing his patients' body parts**. Dr. Henry Cotton would begin with extraction of teeth. If that failed to cure a patient's mental illness, he would remove organs such as the tonsils, stomach, and large intestine.

are you sh*tting me?

FACT 52 👉 **More than a third of Dr. Cotton's patients died.** Shocking, right?

FACT 53 👉 By the end of his career, Dr. Cotton had removed **thousands of tonsils and teeth** from patients at his hospital—a hospital that served a lot of soup.

FACT 54 👉 During the **Great Plague** in 1665, one recommended way to stop the disease was to smoke tobacco. At Eton College in England, boys were paddled for *not* smoking.

FACT 55 👉 Victorian-era women who showed interest in sex were often labeled **mentally ill nymphomaniacs**.

FACT 56 👉 Victorian treatments for nymphomania included enemas, **leech treatments to genitalia**, and even a clitoridectomy, the surgical removal of the clitoris.

FACT 57 👈 The concept of nymphomania was first laid out by the French physician M. D. T. Bienville in his 1771 treatise *Nymphomania, Or a Dissertation Concerning the Furor Uterinus*. Among the behaviors Bienville cited as symptomatic of nymphomania: **dwelling on impure thoughts, reading novels, and eating too much chocolate.**

FACT 58 👈 Victorians believed that **masturbation could lead to insanity, blindness, and death**, which is why at least one British gynecologist at that time, Dr. Isaac Baker Brown, recommended that any woman who masturbated should have her clitoris removed. I say that if God didn't want us to masturbate, He would have made our arms shorter.

FACT 59 👈 Boys who masturbated during the Victorian era risked **having their foreskins sewn up**, with only a small hole left for urination.

FACT 60 👈 **Other Victorian boys had their hands tied to their bedposts during the night or wore straitjacket pajamas to prevent masturbation.**

are you sh*tting me?

FACT 61 👈 Patented in 1876, the Stephenson Spermatic Truss is an antimasturbatory device that **squeezed the penis into a small pouch** that was stretched and strapped down between the legs to prevent erections.

FACT 62 👈 Another device, the **four-pointed penile ring**, is a metal collar lined with spikes that was worn around the penis, effectively thwarting erections.

FACT 63 👈 Wearers of the Bowen Device would have their **pubic hair ripped from the body** should erection occur. Nowadays people pay good money to have their pubes ripped out.

FACT 64 👈 The **penis-cooling device** uses cold water or air to prevent erections.

FACT 65 In an early American pediatric guide, the *Treatise on the Physical and Medical Treatment of Children* (1825), Dr. William Dewees advised expectant mothers in late pregnancy to allow "a young but sufficiently strong puppy" to suckle at their breasts to **toughen the nipples** and improve milk flow in preparation for breast-feeding.

Things That Fall from the Sky

THE FIRST THING I did after researching this chapter was to go online and order one of those umbrella hats. It's not particularly fashionable, I know, and my family now refuses to go anywhere in public with me, but I don't care. I'll be damned if I let falling birds or frozen dung from an airplane toilet take me out and make me the laughingstock of the next life, if there is one.

FACT 66 Blue ice occurs when an airplane's sewage tank or drain tube develops a leak, exposing the **blue waste treatment liquid** from a plane's toilet to freezing temperatures at high altitudes. In most cases, blue ice forms and remains attached to the aircraft's exterior, but it can sometimes break off and plummet to the ground.

FACT 67 In 2007, a Leicester, England, couple was "enjoying a spot of good weather" outside when **a chunk of blue ice hit their home, then struck their heads**. The husband reported that the ice had "a particularly pungent whiff of urine."

FACT 68 Along with being a hazard to those on the ground, **waste leakage** is a safety issue for air travel. In some cases, blue ice has damaged planes, in one instance knocking an engine off a wing.

FACT 69 👉 In 2012, a Long Island couple complained that they were struck with blackish-green fluid that fell from an airplane overhead. The liquid was first thought to be oil but was later **identified as excrement**, presumably from the plane's lavatory.

- -

FACT 70 👉 In 2002, the home of a woman in Armstrong County, Pennsylvania, was **pelted with blue ice**, which landed on her car and her child's swing set, and in the swimming pool. Some melted ice also seeped into her air-conditioning unit.

- -

FACT 71 👉 In 2006, **a large chunk of blue ice ripped a two-foot hole in an elderly couple's roof** in Chino, California, and crashed into their bed, which, luckily, was unoccupied at the time.

- -

FACT 72 👉 Blue ice can fall from the sky with enough force to **crash through roofs and crush cars**.

FACT 73 👉 In February 2013, **a meteor exploded** over the Ural Mountains in Russia. The blast shattered windows and injured nearly eleven hundred people.

FACT 74 👉 Entering Earth's atmosphere at a speed of at least **thirty-three thousand miles per hour**, the ten-ton meteor broke into numerous pieces about twenty miles above the ground.

FACT 75 👉 Small asteroids can also explode with tremendous power, explains Andrew Cheng of the Johns Hopkins Applied Physics Laboratory. "It doesn't take a very large object. A ten-meter-size object **packs the same energy as a nuclear bomb**," Cheng said.

FACT 76 👉 In 1976, **a meteorite entered Earth's atmosphere and exploded** in the skies near the city of Jilin in northeast China. Witnesses confirmed seeing the red fireball split into several pieces before falling to the ground.

are you sh*tting me?

FACT 77 At the meteor's impact site, investigators found **eleven large masses weighing a total of four metric tons**. Now on display in Jilin City, "Meteorite 1" has the honor of being the largest stone meteorite discovered in recent years.

FACT 78 In 1954, a Talladega County, Alabama, woman was **the first recorded human to be hit by a meteorite** when an eight-pound chunk tore through her roof and struck her while she was napping. The woman was not seriously injured.

FACT 79 **Histoplasmosis**, a disease that can affect humans and animals, is caused by a fungus in bird droppings.

FACT 80 When histoplasmosis spores are inhaled, **infection can occur**.

FACT 81 While most infections produce only a **flu-like illness** or no symptoms at all, severe cases of histoplasmosis can cause high fever, blood abnormalities, pneumonia, and even death.

FACT 82 Some areas near the Mississippi and Ohio Rivers show evidence of previous histoplasmosis infection in **up to 80 percent of the population**.

FACT 83 **Pigeon droppings** can contain *E. coli* bacteria and the fungus *Cryptococcus neoformans*. Pigeons can also be carriers of viruses commonly borne by mosquitoes, such as West Nile encephalitis.

FACT 84 Every year in Britain, an estimated two thousand people **catch infections from wild pigeons**. Worse yet, the number of pigeons in Britain is estimated to have doubled in the past five years.

FACT 85 An estimated **thirty to forty thousand wild pigeons** roost in London's Trafalgar Square alone.

 are you sh*tting me?

FACT 86 👈 The dead body of a Dutch skydiver went undiscovered for more than a week in 2012 before it was found by chance in a field. No one in the man's jump group noticed that his **parachute failed to open** or that he did not check in after the jump.

FACT 87 👈 An experienced fifty-one-year-old skydiver was attempting a complex stunt in March 2013 when both his parachutes failed, sending him into a three-minute spin. Despite **hitting the ground at thirty miles per hour**, the man survived with minor injuries.

FACT 88 👈 When both of her chutes failed to open during a 2004 jump, veteran South African skydiver Christine McKenzie fell into **a hundred-mile-per-hour free fall from eleven thousand feet**. Luckily, McKenzie's plummet was broken by power lines, and she suffered only a broken pelvis.

FACT 89 👉 For several days in November 1976, **hundreds of dead blackbirds and pigeons** fell intermittently on the streets of San Luis Obispo, California. The California Department of Fish and Game theorized the birds had been poisoned and were soon proven right: California Polytechnic University admitted to seeding a field near the town with poison grains in the hopes of better controlling the bird population.

FACT 90 👉 On New Year's Eve in 2011, thousands of dead birds fell on the town of Beebe, Arkansas. Preliminary tests showed the birds had died from **blunt-force trauma** before they hit the ground. Investigators believe that the five thousand dead blackbirds, European starlings, and others were flushed from their roosts by local fireworks and were driven to fly lower than usual, where their poor night vision sent them crashing into buildings, trees, and other stationary objects.

FACT 91 👉 After **meat chunks fell from the sky** and struck a Kentucky woman in 1876, analysis revealed the meat to be venison. One professor wrote in the *Louisville Medical News* that the "only plausible theory" for the meaty rain was "the disgorgement of some vultures that were sailing over the spot." In other words, buzzard vomit.

FACT 92 👉 In 1902, clouds from a giant Illinois dust storm blew across the eastern United States, mixed with rain clouds, and later fell as **mud showers**.

FACT 93 👉 During storms, **waterspouts can suck up fish, frogs, and snakes from oceans or lakes**. Strong winds can carry the animals miles inland before dropping them to the ground.

FACT 94 👉 Witnesses from England to India to the United States have reported instances of **fish falling from the sky**.

FACT 95 👉 The United Kingdom's Great Yarmouth has the dubious honor of being named **the country's most likely place for strange objects to fall from the sky**. The British Weather Services cites the instability of the atmosphere and the town's proximity to the North Sea as contributing factors.

FACT 96 👉 In 2002, **hundreds of tiny silver fish** rained upon Great Yarmouth. The fish were fresh but dead.

FACT 97 👉 For two days in 2010, hundreds of small white fish poured onto the town of Lajamanu in Australia's Northern Territory. Though Lajamanu is hundreds of miles from the nearest body of water, this was the **third incident of falling fish** in the town in thirty-six years.

FACT 98 👉 In October 2012, **a two-foot-long leopard shark fell on a golf course** in San Juan Capistrano, California. Experts believe a bird grabbed the shark from the ocean and then dropped it onto the course.

FACT 99 👉 If you think spiders are scary, imagine them falling from the sky. That's what seemed to be happening in February 2013 when **thousands of large spiders descended** upon Santo Antonio da Platina, Brazil. Turns out the spiders weren't falling but dangling from power lines and poles while mating. Which isn't any less frightening.

FACT 100 👉 In 1969, the town of Punta Gorda, Florida, was pelted with "dozens and dozens" of **golf balls falling from the sky** during a rainstorm. Officials theorized that the passing storm had sucked up a golf-ball-filled pond.

are you sh*tting me?

FACT 101 In March 2013, an eight-year-old schoolgirl on a field trip in Berkeley, California, was surprised to discover that her leg had been **pierced with a two-foot-long crossbow bolt** that had fallen from the sky. The girl's injury wasn't life-threatening.

FACT 102 A seven-year-old Wisconsin girl **took a hunting arrow to the back** in 2012 while outside playing. She suffered lung and spleen injuries.

FACT 103 A Manson, Washington, couple narrowly escaped injury in 2007 when **a six-hundred-pound cow fell off a two-hundred-foot cliff** and onto their minivan, causing significant damage.

FACT 104 In 1942, a British forest guard in the Indian Himalayas discovered a frozen lake filled with hundreds of skeletons. The cause of these deaths remained unsolved until 2004, when a National Geographic team examined the bones and determined that the victims had **suffered blows to the head and shoulders** caused by "blunt, round objects about the size of cricket balls." The conclusion: two hundred travelers were crossing the valley in 850 C.E. when they were caught in a deadly hailstorm.

FACT 105 👉 Ninety-two people were killed in Gopalganj, Bangladesh, in 1986 when **grapefruit-size hail** fell during a storm.

FACT 106 👉 The Guinness World Records has designated hail from the Gopalganj storm as being the heaviest ever recorded, at **two pounds**.

FACT 107 👉 The **deadliest hailstorm on record** occurred in 1888 in Moradabad, India, and killed 246 people.

FACT 108 👉 While most of the pollen we inhale doesn't go farther than the shallow portions of our airways, **some tiny fragments can make their way deeper into our respiratory system**. These fragments can be dangerous to anyone with existing respiratory and health issues, including sufferers of asthma, cardiovascular disease, and pneumonia.

are you sh*tting me?

FACT 109   Studies suggest that **pollen fragments can impair health**. One Dutch study showed a "strong association between day-to-day variations in pollen concentrations and deaths from cardiovascular disease, chronic obstructive pulmonary disease, and pneumonia."

FACT 110 In June 2010, a mother holding her baby daughter at Central Park Zoo in New York City was struck by **a large tree branch that snapped and fell thirty feet**. The child was killed instantly; the mother was critically injured but survived.

FACT 111 A Brooklyn, New York, man was killed in February 2010 when **a large branch, weighed down by snow, snapped off a tree** and struck him.

FACT 112 On July 30, 2010, a man was seriously hurt when a **rotting branch** from a large oak tree in New York City's Central Park broke off, fell twenty feet, and hit him.

FACT 113 An expectant mother and her unborn child were both killed in August 2013 when **a huge tree branch fell on them** in a Queens, New York, park.

FACT 114    A study of a Papua New Guinea hospital shows that over a four-year period, 2.5 percent of all admissions were due to people being struck by **falling coconuts**. And you thought it only happened on *Gilligan's Island*.

FACT 115   Falling coconuts can cause blows to the head of a force **greater than one metric ton**, since mature palms can grow up to 115 feet and an unhusked coconut can weigh up to nine pounds.

FACT 116   Though **firing weapons into the sky** is an accepted expression of celebration in parts of the world, the practice has, not surprisingly, led to unintentional killings.

FACT 117   The Centers for Disease Control and Prevention (CDC) cites a Puerto Rican report that concluded that a bullet fired into the skies can return to earth with **enough force to kill a human being**.

FACT 118   The same Puerto Rican study found that **eighteen people were injured and one killed** during that country's 2004 New Year's Eve celebrations.

are you sh*tting me?

FACT 119 🖒 A widely cited study by doctors at a medical center in Los Angeles between 1985 and 1992 identified 118 injuries nationwide believed to have come from **bullets falling from the sky**.

FACT 120 🖒 A seven-year-old Virginia boy was killed in 2013 when **a stray bullet pierced the top of his head** and lodged into the base of his skull. The boy and his family were on their way to a Fourth of July fireworks display when the accident occurred.

FACT 121 🖒 On New Year's Eve in 2010, a four-year-old boy at church with his family died after **a bullet came through the roof** and struck him in the head. A ballistics expert estimated that the shot came from a half mile away.

FACT 122 🖒 A fifteen-year-old Amish girl was killed in 2011 near Wooster, Ohio, after being struck by a bullet fired by a man cleaning his **musket rifle** over a mile away. Who knew a musket rifle could fire a mile?

FACT 123 👉 **Stray bullets** fired during a New Year's celebration killed three people in the Philippines in 2011.

FACT 124 👉 In 2010, a Turkish groom fired an AK-47 into the air at his wedding and **killed three family members** when the bullets returned to earth.

FACT 125 👉 **Celebratory gunfire was blamed for three deaths** in Baghdad after the Iraqi football team defeated Vietnam in 2007's Asia Cup.

FACT 126 👉 **Twenty people were killed** by celebratory gunfire at the end of the Gulf War in 1991.

FACT 127 👉 In July 2013, **a five-by-five-foot piece of a U.S. Air Force C-17 fell off the aircraft** and landed in a San Antonio, Texas, man's backyard. "We saw something drop off from the plane," said one witness, "and shortly after we heard a loud bang." No one was injured.

FACT 128 In September 2012, **a refrigerator-size sheet of metal fell from the sky** and onto a heavily trafficked street in the Seattle suburb of Kent, Washington. The object, a landing gear door from a Boeing 767, fell off the plane and skipped thirty feet on the street before stopping.

FACT 129 In June 2013, a Long Island, New York, man says he was standing outside when **a metal clipboard fell from the sky** and crashed onto the pavement only a few feet away. The clipboard is believed to have fallen from a passing airplane, possibly left by the pilot on the wing.

FACT 130 Any type of precipitation—including snow and fog, and small pieces of dry material—with high levels of nitric and sulfuric acids is considered **"acid rain."**

FACT 131 The biggest cause of acid rain? **The burning of fossil fuels** by automobiles, factories, and coal-fueled power plants— all human activities.

FACT 132 Acid rain causes lakes and streams to **absorb aluminum from the soil,** making bodies of water toxic to fish and other aquatic animals.

FACT 133 By robbing the soil of essential nutrients and releasing aluminum into it, **acid rain makes it hard for trees to absorb water**. It also damages the leaves of trees.

FACT 134 **Volcanic eruptions** can cause fires, damage to existing structures, and changes in climate. However, one of the most deadly parts of an eruption (aside from the molten lava, of course) is the ash, which carries harmful poisonous gases.

FACT 135 The world's deadliest hot-air balloon accident in two decades happened in February 2013 when a **balloon explosion** over southern Egypt dropped twenty-one passengers and crew a thousand feet to the ground, killing nineteen.

are you sh*tting me?

FACT 136 In 2013, a young man's body was found on the sidewalk in west London. Authorities believe he was a stowaway who **hid inside the landing gear** of a flight from Angola, and that due to hypothermia and lack of oxygen, the man was either already dead or near death when the airplane's landing gear door opened for the descent and he fell out.

FACT 137 Since 1947, there have been **ninety-six identified cases** in which people tried to hide in an airplane's wheel housing. Less than 25 percent of those stowaways survived.

FACT 138 In June 2012, searchers found the body of the sixth and final member of a family whose private plane crashed near Tampa. Investigators believe thirteen-year-old Boston Bramlage was **thrown from the aircraft before impact**. His body was found half a mile from the crash site.

FACT 139 In April 2013, a Sioux Falls, South Dakota, couple was surprised when **a frozen turkey vulture landed with a thud** on their front porch. Evidently, the bird's wings had frozen after it flew through a snowstorm. It later thawed and flew off again.

Alleged Alien Abductions

NO MATTER WHAT YOU might believe about reports of people being abducted by aliens, you have to admit two things: one, the people who report them sure seem to believe they happened; two, their stories, real or imagined, are frightening.

I wonder if alien abductions are a thing on other planets, too. I wonder if right now in some faraway alien land, a little green guy is trying to cover up a weekend tryst with his little green girlfriend by telling his wife that he was abducted by earthlings with tiny eyes who tied him to an exam table and prodded his alien corn hole for days with strange otherworldly tools.

FACT 140 One of the first alleged alien abduction cases to gain widespread interest was that of Brazilian farmer Antônio Villas-Boas, who claimed in 1957 that he was taken aboard an egg-shaped UFO and **forced to have sex with a naked female entity** whom the aliens wanted him to impregnate.

FACT 141 After his abduction, Villas-Boas **suffered from nausea, loss of appetite, sleeplessness, and headaches**. He died in 1992, never having retracted his story.

are you sh*tting me?

FACT 142 👉 The 1961 case of Betty and Barney Hill is one of the most famous and well-documented claims of alien abduction. The New Hampshire couple say they **encountered a UFO during a road trip** but could remember no other details of the rest of their journey. Their trip also took hours longer than it should have, time for which the Hills could not account.

FACT 143 👉 After the encounter, both Hills experienced **anxiety and disturbing dreams**. Betty's dreams included being taken into a spacecraft by gray-skinned men in military uniforms, then being given an examination and pregnancy test by an alien doctor.

FACT 144 👉 Betty Hill also dreamed that aliens showed her a star map detailed with **interplanetary trade routes** and including our own sun. After Hill was able to reproduce a diagram of the map from memory, an amateur astronomer matched it to a section of our solar system.

FACT 145 👉 A 2013 survey by the Huffington Post showed that almost half of respondents are open to the idea that **alien spacecraft are observing our planet**. Probably because those respondents are aliens on spacecraft observing our planet.

FACT 146 👉 Many psychologists believe that **alien abduction claims are dreams or hallucinations** that are triggered by a familiarity with other people's similar accounts.

FACT 147 👉 A South Ashburnham, Massachusetts, woman named Betty Andreasson claimed in 1957 that she was abducted by aliens and taken onto a spaceship. Andreasson says her **alien captors communicated via telepathy** and subjected her to medical tests. The good news: her cholesterol and blood pressure were normal.

FACT 148 👉 Andreasson's case was studied by Mutual UFO Network (MUFON) founder and investigator Ray Fowler, who put Betty under hypnosis to verify her claims. Fowler concluded that Andreasson was "either the most accomplished liar and actress the world had ever seen, or else she had **really gone through this ordeal**."

are you sh*tting me?

FACT 149 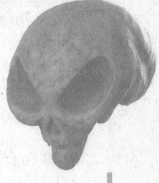   Under hypnosis, Andreasson claimed the **aliens implanted a foreign object** in her skull.

FACT 150 👉   Andreasson said the aliens told her the experiments they were conducting were to "prepare for some kind of **planetary revelation**."

FACT 151 👉   Travis Walton was an Arizona logger who **went missing for several days** in November 1975. His colleagues were initially suspected of having killed Walton and dumped him in the woods, but they maintained that Walton had been knocked out by a beam of light from a UFO and then vanished.

FACT 152 👉   Walton turned up five days later and alleged that he had been **abducted by aliens and taken aboard their spacecraft**, where he was subjected to a medical examination. In other words, he went on a five-day malt liquor bender.

FACT 153 👉 One psychiatrist who examined Walton said, "This young man is not lying. There is no collusion involved. **He really believes these things.**"

FACT 154 👉 Both Walton and his colleagues **passed numerous polygraph tests** that questioned the events of their abduction account. None of the men has ever changed his story.

FACT 155 👉 In 1976, four men camping in Maine's Allagash Wilderness claimed they were in a canoe on a lake when a UFO appeared and shot **a huge beam of light** down at them. They regained consciousness several hours later with no recollection of what had occurred.

FACT 156 👉 **Under hypnosis**, two of the men claimed they had been having other visitations by alien creatures and abduction experiences since early childhood. All of the Allagash men took and passed lie detector tests about their claims.

are you sh*tting me?

FACT 157 Some purported victims of alien abduction have reported that their captors inserted **tiny implants** inside them—sending long needles into their brains through their nasal passages to place the implants.

FACT 158 In the 1980s, a group of alleged alien abductees went through a battery of psychological tests and were found to be suffering from **post-traumatic stress disorder**. Dr. Elizabeth Slater, a psychologist, said that the finding were "not inconsistent with the possibility that reported UFO abductions have, in fact, occurred."

FACT 159 Kirsan Ilyumzhinov, the former leader of the Republic of Kalmykia in the Russian Federation, claimed on a 2010 talk show that aliens took him from his Moscow home in 1997 and **gave him a tour of their ship**.

FACT 160 In 1973, Charles Hickson and Calvin Parker said they were fishing on the Pascagoula River in Mississippi when **they were levitated onto an alien spaceship**, where they were subjected to a medical examination by humanoid creatures with claws like a lobster.

FACT 161 👉 Air Force sergeant Charles Moody claimed that on a night in August 1975, he saw a UFO flying toward him in the New Mexico desert. Moody tried to escape but his car wouldn't move. His next recollection was of the UFO flying away. When Moody arrived home, **he found that many hours had passed**.

FACT 162 👉 British police officer Alan Godfrey claimed that he was on patrol one night in November 1980 when he saw a **large UFO hovering over the road** ahead of him. As he attempted to make a sketch of the craft, there was a tremendous flash of light. His next recollection was of being farther along the road, but the UFO had vanished.

FACT 163 👉 Later, under regression hypnosis, Godfrey remembered being taken to an enclosed space and meeting a **bearded man called Yosef** who was accompanied by five small robot-like creatures.

FACT 164 👉 **The list of people who've claimed to see UFOs includes two former presidents: Ronald Reagan and Jimmy Carter.**

FACT 165 In 1974, former president Richard Nixon allegedly took comedian Jackie Gleason to Homestead Air Force Base in Florida and showed him the **wreckage of a flying saucer** and remains of an extraterrestrial.

FACT 166 A

folk tale dating

from 1645 tells

of a teenage girl

in Cornwall, England, who reported

being **attacked by small aliens** and

carried to a "castle in the air," where

she was raped.

FACT 167 In his 1954 book, *The White Sands Incident*, Daniel Fry claims that he was abducted by an alien craft that took him from New Mexico to New York City and back in **half an hour**.

FACT 168  Fry said that his alien hosts claimed to be descendants of an **ancient race of earthlings** who had abandoned the planet after a war between the lost continents of Lemuria and Atlantis.

FACT 169 On December 3, 1967, policeman Herbert Schirmer was on patrol near Ashland, Nebraska, when, he says, he saw a UFO. When Schirmer arrived home later that night, he felt ill and had **inexplicable red welts** on his neck. Also, twenty minutes were missing from his police log.

 are you sh*tting me?

FACT 170 👉 Under hypnosis later, Schirmer recalled being taken aboard an alien spaceship whose occupants told him that they came from a neighboring galaxy, but had **hidden bases on Earth**, one of which was underwater in Florida. Naturally. If aliens are anywhere in this country, it's Florida.

FACT 171 👉 Harvard researcher and author Susan Clancy says that people who allege alien abductions aren't crazy, but that they have "**a tendency to fantasize and to hold unusual beliefs and ideas**. They believe . . . in things like UFOs, ESP, astrology . . . [and] also have in common a rash of disturbing experiences for which they are seeking an explanation. For them, alien abduction is the best fit."

FACT 172 ☞ Clancy and other scientists believe these experiences can be attributed to **sleep paralysis**, a condition in which a person is aware of his surroundings but unable to move.

- -

FACT 173 ☞ In November 2011, the White House released an official response to two petitions asking the U.S. government to acknowledge formally that aliens have visited Earth and to disclose any intentional withholding of government interactions with extraterrestrial beings. According to the response, "The U.S. government has **no evidence that any life exists outside our planet**, or that an extraterrestrial presence has contacted or engaged any member of the human race."

5

Disgusting Food from Around the World

DO YOU EVER WONDER how certain foods became acceptable to eat? I do. I wonder who was the first guy to dig up a beet and say, "Y'know, I'll bet this red, dirt-covered root that looks like a nut sack is delicious. I think I'll munch on it." Or who was the first Scandinavian to find a dead fish on the beach and say to his friend, "Hey, Sven, check this out—let's cut the head off this fish, pull out its guts, stuff it with oxtail and pelican dick, then cover the whole thing in horse shit and bury it in the mud to fester for two years until it's nice and rotten, then dig it up, grab some beers, and chow down."

I suppose it's hungry people who come up with this stuff. I hope I never get that hungry.

FACT 174  The Icelandic dish *hákarl* is **fermented, dried basking shark**. A beheaded and gutted shark is buried in the ground for three months and then dried for five months before being eaten with pickled ram's testicles.

- -

FACT 175 *Casu marzu*, a Sardinian delicacy, is made with both **rancid cheese and live maggots**. That's right: maggots. Live ones.

FACT 176 If you're in Norway and order *smalahove*, the server will bring you a **boiled, salted, and dried lamb's head** with the brain removed. A good server will remind you to eat the ears and eyes first, as they are the tastiest parts. An excellent server will bring you a barf bag and extra napkins.

FACT 177 Some South Americans enjoy eating *cuy*, or **guinea pig**. The low-fat, tender meat is often served whole with the animal's head still attached.

FACT 178 *Cuy* is said to be most delicious when **slow-cooked on a rotisserie and served with hot sauce**.

FACT 179 The Scandinavian dish *lappkok* is made with **reindeer blood and bone marrow** mixed with white or rye flour.

FACT 180 Scotland's famed *haggis* is a cooked **sheep's stomach** stuffed with a mixture of its pluck (lungs, heart, tongue, and/or liver), oatmeal, suet, and spices.

FACT 181 🐴   The UK dish **black (or blood) pudding** is technically a sausage made of animal (usually pork) blood, spices, fat, and oatmeal or other grains.

FACT 182 🐴   If you know that **donkey and horse are eaten throughout Italy**, you won't be surprised to hear about *stracotto d'asino*, a stew made with donkey meat and frequently used as pasta sauce. Also not surprising: it tastes like ass!

FACT 183 🐴   *Shirako*, a Japanese delicacy, is made from the **semen of fish and mollusks**, and has a custard-like texture when cooked.

FACT 184 🐴   Looking for the perfect way to serve a **calf's head**, or as the French call it, *tête de veau*? Try it with mushrooms, rooster combs, kidneys, and calf sweetbreads.

FACT 185 🐴   *Ptcha* is a jelly made from **calves' feet** that is enjoyed primarily by Ashkenazi Jews.

FACT 186 🐴   Don't order the *paardenrookvlees* in the Netherlands unless you're down with eating **smoked horse meat**.

FACT 187 👈 Greeks enjoy *kokoretsi*: **lamb or goat intestines wrapped around seasoned organs**, then skewered and cooked on a spit.

FACT 188 👈 Often referred to as "insect caviar," Mexico's *escamoles* are the **larvae of ants**.

FACT 189 👈 Harvesting *escamole* from the roots of the agave and maguey plants is no easy chore. Pickers can endure **painful ant bites** as they dig for the larvae.

FACT 190 👈 Made of fermented fish, the Nordic dish *surströmming* smells so bad, **it's usually consumed outdoors**.

FACT 191 👈 The next time you're in Kyrgyzstan, try the *kumis*, a carbonated, mildly alcoholic drink made from the **fermented milk of a female horse**.

FACT 192 👈 If you do drink *kumis*, make sure there is a bathroom nearby, as the drink has a **laxative effect**.

FACT 193 🖝 In Vietnam, *tiết canh*, or **raw blood soup**, is a protein-rich breakfast dish made from the uncooked blood of ducks, geese, or pigs, served with peanuts and herbs on top.

FACT 194 🖝 If you're looking to catch the **H5N1 bird flu virus**, eating *tiết canh* is a good way to do it.

FACT 195 🖝 **Cat meat** is a traditional food in much of Africa and Asia.

FACT 196 🖝 **Corn smut** is not porn made in Iowa, but a disease of the corn plant that replaces the normal kernels of the cobs with large distorted tumors similar to mushrooms. Considered a pest in the United States, corn smut is a delicacy in Mexico.

FACT 197 🖝 To craft *casu marzu*, makers encourage the *Piophilia casei* (cheese fly) to **lay eggs** in their sheep's-milk cheeses. The eggs then hatch into maggots and release an enzyme during their digestion that causes the cheese to ferment.

are you sh*tting me?

FACT 198 👉 Because of European Union health regulations, *casu marzu* has been **outlawed for years**.

- -

FACT 199 👉 *Lutefisk* is a traditional dish of the Nordic countries made from **dried whitefish and soda lye** (*lut*). Its name literally means "lye fish."

- -

FACT 200 👉 In some Andean cultures, **frog juice is believed to cure a variety of conditions**, from asthma to low sex drive. The drink is made from nectar, white bean juices, aloe vera, malt, and—yes— a whole frog, all mixed together in a blender.

- -

FACT 201 👉 **Live octopus** is a delicacy in some parts of Asia. Smaller octopi can be served "cut into bite-sized, still-wriggling pieces, suction cups and all, or slurped squirming, whole."

- -

FACT 202 👉 Indonesians snack on **stinkbugs**, which are said to taste like bitter unsalted sunflower seeds.

- -

FACT 203 👉 *Nozki*—Polish for "cold feet"—is **seasoned pig's feet** set in gelatin. No one could blame you for having *nozki* about eating *nozki*.

FACT 204 The lucky diners who get to eat live octopus might also enjoy the **suction cups** sticking to the insides of their throats as they swallow.

FACT 205 In Thailand, **bat paste** is a delicacy made from live bats that are boiled, roasted, chopped into paste, and mixed with herbs and spices.

FACT 206 Here's one way to overcome a fear of spiders: eat them. Cambodians dine on **fried tarantulas**, a food that became popular during famines in that country in the 1970s. This yummy snack is crunchy on the outside and gooey on the inside—much like a chicken dish I made for dinner the other night.

FACT 207 If you order **drunken shrimp** in China, you'll be served a crustacean that is still alive but stunned from being soaked in liquor. You might want to be soaked in liquor, too, before eating it.

FACT 208 The next time you're in southern Africa, try the *mopane*, a **crisp, dried caterpillar** that is an important source of protein for millions of people on that continent.

 are you sh*tting me?

FACT 209 👉 In Japan, **one American dollar will score you a tuna eyeball** for lunch.

FACT 210 👉 Some Asian cultures are fond of **dried lizards**, which are used to flavor soup and for medicinal purposes.

FACT 211 👉 *Khash* is a Farsi word meaning "head and hoof" and is also the name of an Armenian dish made with—you guessed it—the **head, feet, and stomach of cows**.

FACT 212 👉 Rich in protein, **chapulines** (grasshoppers) are a favorite snack in Oaxaca, Mexico.

FACT 213 👉 Uncooked *chapulines* are **dangerous to eat**, as they can carry roundworms.

FACT 214 👉 **Steeped snake wine** is made by pickling a poisonous snake in a large jar of rice wine. The snake's venom is rendered harmless by the wine's high alcohol content.

FACT 215 🖙 **Camel meat** is a delicacy in the Middle East.

FACT 216 🖙 The **camel hump** is the most tender and fatty part of the animal, making it the sought-after part to eat.

FACT 217 🖙 Chef and food writer Anissa Helou tried camel hump in Abu Dhabi and describes its taste as a "**cross between beef and lamb**. It was from a baby camel—older camels will taste dry and tough."

FACT 218 🖙 A delicacy in Mexico, *chinicuiles* are **caterpillar worms** harvested from the roots of maguey and agave plants. Their meat is protein-rich and highly nutritious.

FACT 219 🖙 *Pani ca' meusa*, or **bread with spleen**, is a specialty of Sicilian street food vendors. The sandwich is made of cheese, lemon, and deep-fried veal spleen.

FACT 220 🖙 *Hasma* is a Chinese dessert ingredient made from the tissue surrounding the **fallopian tubes of frogs**.

FACT 221 🕮 If you ever say to yourself, **"Ya know, I'm really craving some pork butthole right now,"** get yourself to Namibia, where unwashed, lightly cooked warthog anus is a delicacy. Just don't forget your toothbrush.

FACT 222 🕮 A traditional favorite in Greenland, *kiviak* is made by **stuffing the carcass of a seal with dead birds** and burying it in the spring or summer. At Christmas, the fermented meat is dug up so holiday revelers can bite off the birds' heads and suck out the jellied guts.

FACT 223 🕮 Indonesia is home to the **cobra burger**, which isn't just a catchy name: it's made with real cobra meat.

FACT 224 🕮 Many Taiwanese consider consuming **cobra eggs and embryos** good for your health.

FACT 225 🕮 In Japan, consuming frog is thought to **improve virility**.

FACT 226   **Penises of animals** such as dogs, donkeys, and oxen are routinely consumed in China, as they are thought to have medicinal properties.

FACT 227   If you've ever wondered a **scorpion** might taste like, visit southern China, where the fearsome arthropod is routinely eaten fried or in soup.

FACT 228   If you're offered a "pinkie" to eat in Asia, know that you're getting a **baby mouse or rat** that's been deep-fried or grilled whole.

FACT 229   In Madagascar, poachers illegally kill endangered lemurs and sell the bodies to restaurants as **"luxury bush meat."**

FACT 230   Diners who order frog sashimi in Japan are offered the chance to **eat the still-beating heart** of the creature.

6

Boogers

OLD JOKE: WHAT'S THE difference between boogers and broccoli? Kids won't eat broccoli. Neither will some adults, which makes me wonder if they eat boogers, too. Actually, they do, as you are about to discover. I discovered it for myself on the Tube in London last year when I saw an attractive, well-dressed woman absentmindedly pick her nose and then eat it. I'm guessing she was a tourist who couldn't face another English dinner, so she decided to snack on the train. Bless.

FACT 231 The technical name for **using one's finger to pick boogers** is *rhinotillexis*. As opposed to using your toes, which has no technical name but is one hell of a trick.

FACT 232 The act of **eating the boogers** is called *mucophagy*.

FACT 233 About 70 percent of people admit to picking their nose; 30 percent of those confess to **eating the boogers they pick**. Everyone else sticks them under the chair or on the bathroom wall.

FACT 234 The average person picks his nose **five times every hour**.

FACT 235 Boogers are green because they are **rich in iron**.

FACT 236 👉 The color of your boogers can be a clue to your health. **Green or yellow boogers indicate illness**. Black boogers are heavy with dust and dirt. Orange boogers mean you eat too many Cheetos.

FACT 237 👉 **Red or brown boogers contain blood**, which could mean you're picking too hard or too frequently.

FACT 238 👉 One Austrian lung specialist, Dr. Friedrich Bischinger, has gained notoriety by recommending that kids eat their boogers to help **strengthen their immune systems**.

FACT 239 👉 Bischinger recommends that you **use fingers for nose-picking** because "you can get to places you just can't reach with a handkerchief, keeping your nose far cleaner." Never shake hands with this man.

FACT 240 👉 Other medical professionals counter that inserting germ-covered fingers into the nose is a bad idea, as it **introduces more bacteria** into the body.

FACT 241 👉 Bacteria thrive in the **warm, moist atmosphere of the nose**, where they can cause infection and illness.

FACT 242 👉 Your body produces about a **quart of snot every day**, most of which is swallowed. The rest of it is hocked up by baseball players during games.

FACT 243 👉 The purpose of snot, or mucus in the nose, is to **protect the lungs** by trapping particles we inhale, such as dust, dirt, pollen, and smoke.

FACT 244 👉 If **foreign particles** reach the lungs, they can cause irritation and possibly infection, as well as breathing difficulty.

FACT 245 👉 **Cilia**, or hairs inside the nose, work in tandem with snot to move trapped particles to the front of the nose or back of the throat.

FACT 246 👉 Boogers are formed when **snot and trapped debris** clump together.

FACT 247 👉 **Sneezes** leave the body at nearly a hundred miles per hour.

FACT 248 👉 Every sneeze helps us by expelling **thousands of germs**, including bacteria and viruses, from our bodies.

FACT 249 👉 Stifling a sneeze can cause middle and inner ear damage, including a **ruptured eardrum**.

FACT 250 👉 Snot is disgusting, but it serves an important purpose: **to flush germs from the body before they can spread**. We get stuffy when we have colds because the body produces extra snot to fight the illness.

FACT 251 👉 When you cry, **your nose runs** because your tears drain through tear ducts that empty into your nose, mixing with the mucus already there.

FACT 252 👉 When you breathe in cold air, **the blood vessels inside your nose dilate**, warming the air and producing more mucus, creating a runny nose.

FACT 253 👉 Colds are the most **common illness among children** and typically last about a week.

FACT 254 👉 On average, **preschool-age children have about nine colds per year**, while adolescents and adults have about seven colds per year. Lucky kindergartners average twelve colds per year.

FACT 255 👉 The face fly lives on farm animals and **feeds on boogers, tears, spit, poop, and blood**.

FACT 256 👉 In 2008, a UK man **died from a nosebleed** brought on by his compulsive nose-picking habit.

Stoopid Criminals

YOU'VE HEARD THE WORD *schadenfreude*, right? The literal translation from German is "harm joy," but the word means to take satisfaction at the misfortunes of others. It's not usually a nice thing to do, but when it comes to idiots who try to break the law but fail miserably and hilariously, I will make an exception. In other words, laugh it up! But be afraid, too— these people walk among us.

FACT 257 👉 In May 2013, two identity thieves were arrested in Fort Lauderdale, Florida, after posting photos of themselves on **Instagram** enjoying a fancy steak dinner on their victim's dime. The picture was used as evidence in court to identify the thieves.

FACT 258 👉 In 2008, Joseph Goetz's attempt to rob a bank fell apart after the first teller fainted and the next two didn't have any cash in their drawers. Goetz left in a fury, **promising to write an angry letter** to the bank for bad service.

FACT 259 👉 In 2008, two men in Sydney, Australia, were arrested and one was hospitalized after attempting to rob a nightclub during a monthly bikers' meeting. Oops. **The would-be robbers were beaten by dozens of bikers** until police arrived.

FACT 260 🖘 **An Augusta, Georgia, man was arrested for forgery in 2007 after he tried to open a bank account with a $1 million bill—a bill that doesn't exist.**

FACT 261 🖘 A Marin County, California, man was arrested in 2009 for driving a stolen car to court—while he was on trial for stealing another car! The thief was caught after **courthouse bystanders noticed that dogs had been left in the vehicle on a hot day** and alerted police.

FACT 262 🖘 In 2008, an Ontario, Canada, man telephoned a local convenience store **to ask how much money was in the register**. When the would-be robber arrived at the store, police were waiting and arrested him.

FACT 263 🖘 Polish author Krystian Bala was convicted in 2007 of murdering a man in Wrocław in 2000. Bala might have gotten away with it had he not **written a novel** in 2003 that was eerily similar to the unsolved case, tipping police to investigate.

FACT 264 👉 The expression **sent up the river**, which means "going to jail," dates back to the 1800s when criminals were sent up the Hudson River to Sing Sing Prison in Ossining, New York.

FACT 265 👉 In 2007, a robbery suspect in Denton, Texas, **spent ten hours in a narrow drainage pipe** after getting stuck there while trying to hide from pursuing police.

FACT 266 👉 Did you hear the one about the hit-and-run driver who was caught after leaving his **false teeth at the scene of a crash**? It's not a joke; it happened in Sacramento, California, in 2011.

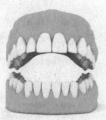

FACT 267 👉 In 2004, ninety-two-year-old J. L. Hunter Rountree became the **oldest person** in U.S. history to be convicted of bank robbery. Rountree was sentenced to twelve years in prison for robbing a Texas bank.

FACT 268 👉 If you want to get caught robbing a bank, just **write your holdup note** on the back of one of your own checks or deposit slips. It happens about forty-five times a year in the United States, according to the FBI.

FACT 269 👉   A man **claiming to have a bomb** burst into a radio station in Wanganui, New Zealand, in 1996 and demanded that the DJ play "The Rainbow Connection" by Kermit the Frog.

FACT 270 👉   Like beef? So do two Spring Valley, California, geniuses who pilfered a commercial freezer in 1996. Unfortunately for them, the freezer belonged to an animal hospital, and the "meat" they stole wasn't steak and chicken but the **frozen corpses of cats and dogs**.

FACT 271 👉   In 1993, convicted serial killer Randy Kraft filed a $60 million libel lawsuit against publishers of a book about his crime spree. He argued that *Angel of Darkness* portrayed him as a "sick, twisted" man "without any moral values." Kraft had been convicted for the **sexual torture murders** of sixteen men, though authorities believe he may have been involved in more killings.

FACT 272 👉   In 2007, a Woodland, California, dentist lost his license and was charged with sexual battery after he was accused of fondling the breasts of twenty-seven female patients. The dentist claimed that the **fondling was an approved treatment for jaw problems** until authorities noted that he performed it only on women, not men.

FACT 273 👉 A Grapevine, Texas, man was arrested in 2008 for impersonating an undercover cop after he pulled over cars using police lights and showed drivers a **Chipotle gift card** with the word *police* scratched into it as a badge.

FACT 274 👉 Two men in Filyro, Greece, were busted in 2007 after turning a Greek Orthodox nunnery into a **pot farm**. The men pretended to be gardeners, volunteering to help the nuns with their grounds.

FACT 275 👉 In Slidell, Louisiana, a group of Krispy Kreme Doughnut truck thieves was caught in 2002 when police followed a **trail of doughnuts** to the perpetrators, who didn't realize that their "loot" was falling out of the vehicle's open back door. Krispy Kreme Doughnut trail—that's like the bat signal for cops.

FACT 276   When two New Jersey women were caught shoplifting in October 2013, they fled the store and left behind not only the stolen goods but also **an eight-month-old infant**. The women were caught in the parking lot and arrested for theft, child endangerment, and possession of heroin.

FACT 277   Two men fleeing police in a high-speed chase in March 2010 abandoned their car and jumped a high fence, which—unfortunately for the men—was **around a women's prison**, where they were caught and arrested.

FACT 278   Bank employees in Fort Worth, Texas, became suspicious in 2008 when a man tried to cash a personal check to **start a record business**. Perhaps it was the amount of the check that clued them in: $360 billion. The man was arrested for forgery.

FACT 279   Here's a tip, job seekers: don't apply for work at a store using your real name and address if you're **going to rob the place**. That's what an Ocala, Florida, man did in July 2013. He didn't get the job, but he did get arrested for burglary and theft.

FACT 280 When a Murfreesboro, Tennessee, man called police in August 2013 to report the theft of his safe, he also told them what was inside the missing safe: a large amount of **marijuana and drug money**. That's when the police told him that he was under arrest.

FACT 281 Minutes after being released from jail on another charge in August 2013, a Chandler, Arizona, man stole an ambulance from a **police station parking lot** because he didn't want to walk home. He was quickly located by GPS and returned to jail, where his bed was likely still warm.

FACT 282 Investigators believe that thieves who **broke into a Hooters restaurant** in San Diego in 2013 stole the jukebox because they mistook it for an ATM. They likely realized their mistake when they tried to make a withdrawal and Warrant's "Cherry Pie" started playing.

are you sh*tting me?

FACT 283 👉 Police in Cassatt, South Carolina, were able to catch a convenience store burglar in July 2013 by following a **trail of Cheetos** to his home.

FACT 284 👉 In March 2013, a Jonesboro, Arkansas, woman suspected of DUI was arrested when she tried to **flee police on a battery-powered toy truck** after crashing her car.

FACT 285 👉 A convenience store robber in Euless, Texas, was busted in 2005 after **leaving his wallet at the scene of the crime**. Police didn't even have to track the man: they just called and told him he could pick up his wallet at the police station's lost and found. The man showed up and was immediately arrested. Said one officer, "We don't even have a lost and found."

8

Torture Devices

IF YOU ARE ONE of these people who believe that humans are inherently good, I'm about to challenge that notion. I'm no misanthrope, but the methods we've invented to hurt each other over the centuries are just plain barbaric and evil. I'm not saying some of the victims didn't deserve it, but damn, what happened to good old simple execution? Couldn't all that creativity have been used in more productive ways, like making an Internet that doesn't go out when I'm on a book deadline?

FACT 286   Used during the Dutch Revolt (1568–1648), **rat torture** involved trapping rats under a bowl on a prisoner's stomach, then heating the bowl's exterior to force the rats to eat through the victim's flesh to try to escape.

FACT 287 🖝   Victims of the **iron chair** were strapped into a chair covered in iron spikes, then pulled slowly tighter into the chair until the spikes pierced their skin. Fires could also be lit underneath the chair to encourage cooperation or make the execution more interesting.

FACT 288 🖝   The breast ripper (also called the iron spider) used **clawlike iron tongs**—often blazing hot—to rip a female victim's breasts from her body.

FACT 289 🖝   Popularized in sixteenth-century Bavaria, **the breast ripper was used on women** charged with adultery, blasphemy, self-abortion, or witchcraft.

FACT 290 👉 Crocodile tongs had jagged, teeth-like edges and were used to **clamp onto a victim's penis** and pull his flesh apart.

FACT 291 👉 Republican marriage, in which a naked man and woman were **tied together and drowned**, was an alleged form of execution during France's Reign of Terror.

FACT 292 👉 Used in Europe throughout the Middle Ages, the breaking wheel featured victims "**tied to a large wooden wheel**, which was rotated slowly while the executioner struck down on their limbs with an iron bar or hammer, breaking the bones."

FACT 293 👉 Breaking wheel torture was usually **carried out in public**, and victims' broken bodies were left on display afterward. Those who didn't die during the torture would suffer for days before dying of dehydration or shock.

FACT 294 👉 The breaking wheel was used in eighteenth-century America to **punish slaves** who tried to revolt.

FACT 295 👉 Until it was outlawed in 1905, *ling chi* was used as a method of execution in China. Known as death by a thousand cuts, *ling chi* involved an executioner **slowly slicing off body parts**, prolonging the suffering of the condemned.

FACT 296 👉 For centuries, the garrote was used to execute criminals in Spain. Victims were **tied to a stake** with a loop of rope placed around their necks. A rod in the loop would be turned to tighten the rope until the person asphyxiated.

FACT 297 👉 Until as recently as 1940, Spain also employed a variation of the garrote in which a **metal spike** was driven into the victim's spinal cord as the loop tightened.

FACT 298 👉 Considered more humane than **burning at the stake**, execution by garrote was generally reserved for heretics who had confessed their crimes. The method was popular during the Spanish Inquisition.

 are you sh*tting me?

FACT 299   The most recent recorded use of garrote was in 1975 during Franco's regime in Spain; a student was executed but was **later proved innocent** of his crime.

FACT 300 **Execution by boiling** was used throughout Europe and Asia until the seventeenth century. The victim was either placed in boiling water or oil, or made to sit in a cauldron full of cold liquid as it was heated to boiling.

FACT 301 In Europe, boiling was used throughout the Middle Ages to execute poisoners and forgers. More recently, the Uzbek government is reported to have **boiled several people** who opposed the political regime.

FACT 302 Ancient Romans practiced the method of *Damnatio ad bestias* or **"condemnation to beasts"**: the execution of live prisoners, often early Christians, by feeding them alive to large animals.

FACT 303 Along with Christians, other offenders who suffered death by beasts included **military deserters, sorcerers, and kidnappers**.

FACT 304 👉 Though less common than other methods, execution by sawing was used in Europe, ancient Rome, the Middle East, and parts of Asia. The condemned was **hung upside down and sawed vertically in two**, starting at the groin. In other words, they fought the saw but the saw won.

FACT 305 👉 Because blood continued to flow to the brain during sawing, the victim is believed to have **remained alive** for much of this agonizing process.

FACT 306 👉 **The notoriously cruel Roman emperor Caligula had those who had fallen out of his favor sawed in half across the torso** while he watched and dined.

FACT 307 👉 From the fourteenth through nineteenth centuries, anyone in England who committed high treason faced execution by **hanging, drawing, and quartering**. The accused would first be hung to near death and disemboweled. Then his genitals would be removed and the body cut into four pieces.

FACT 308 🖝   In 1606, **Guy Fawkes** was sentenced to death by hanging, drawing, and quartering. During the hanging, Fawkes somehow escaped the scaffold but broke his neck in the process. His body was quartered anyway, with all the parts later displayed for the public.

FACT 309 🖝   Bodies of executed criminals were often displayed publicly in chains or hung in metal cages as a way to warn other possible perpetrators. The process, used predominantly in England, was known as **gibbeting**.

FACT 310 🖝   Travelers were often greeted with the sight of gibbets with bodies inside, which were **placed along roads** to deter highway robbery and piracy.

FACT 311 🖝   While most gibbeting was carried out with dead bodies, some lucky criminals were left alive in the gibbet to **die slowly of dehydration**.

FACT 312 🖝   The ancient Greeks practiced a particularly sadistic form of execution known as the brazen bull. The accused would be **locked inside a hollow bronze bull**. A fire was then lit under the bull, and the victim would slowly roast to death inside.

FACT 313 👉 **The bull itself was designed to mimic a real animal. Plumes of smoke escaped through the bull's snout, and a system of tubes made the victim's cries sound like a bellowing beast**.

FACT 314 👉 According to legend, Emperor Hadrian condemned the martyr Saint Eustace and his family to die **inside a brazen bull**.

FACT 315 👉 The **heretic's fork** was a double-sided iron tool that was belted around a victim's neck, causing one end of the fork to pierce the underside of the chin, and the other end to pierce the top of the chest. Any attempt to move caused the wearer more extensive damage.

FACT 316 👉 The medieval torture device called the **Judas cradle** was a large wooden stool with a pyramid-shaped seat. The condemned was suspended over the pyramid and either dropped or lowered slowly until the seat penetrated the vagina or rectum. In either case: ouch.

are you sh*tting me?

FACT 317  Sometimes victims of the Judas cradle had weights strapped to their feet to **intensify the pain**.

FACT 318 Long before it was a rock band, the **iron maiden** was an upright coffin-like device filled with internal spikes on its walls and door. An unfortunate victim would be placed standing inside and couldn't move without being stabbed.

FACT 319 The exterior of the iron maiden was usually **carved to look like a woman**, hence the name.

FACT 320 **Immurement**, or enclosing someone within a wall while still alive, was a rumored medieval torture method.

FACT 321 Victims of immurement **die slowly** of dehydration or hunger.

FACT 322 The **thumbscrew** was a medieval torture device that crushed the victim's fingers and hands as a wooden or metal plate was slowly screwed down. The plate was sometimes stippled with metal studs or nails to pierce the nail beds and inflict more pain.

FACT 323 A square wooden frame with pulley-operated rollers, the **rack** was often used in interrogations. The victim was tied spread-eagled to the rack, which would slowly be extended to pull apart ligaments, joints, and bones. On the bright side, it probably felt good for the first couple of minutes.

FACT 324 Used against homosexuals, blasphemers, and women, the pear of anguish was **a mutilating device inserted into the anus, mouth, or vagina** and slowly opened. Here's hoping they disinfected the thing between uses.

FACT 325 👉 Another favorite of the Spanish Inquisition, the head crusher was a torture device that **held the victim's head between a metal cap and a bar underneath the chin**. A screw at the top of the cap was used to tighten the device slowly to crush the victim's skull and jaw.

FACT 326 👉 **Head-crusher torture sessions** typically lasted for several hours to deliver maximum pain. Occasionally the victim's eyeballs would pop out.

FACT 327 👉 Primarily used in the Middle East and Africa in the Middle Ages, flaying was the act of suspending a victim from a pole and slowly **peeling off his skin from head to toe**. Most victims died before the torture was finished.

FACT 328 👉 Some flaying victims were **boiled or purposely sunburned for added fun** before their skin was removed.

FACT 329 👉 Similar to the breast ripper, the Spanish spider was a chain attached to a wall with spider-like claws at the end, which were sometimes heated. The claws would be latched on to a woman's breast and the torturer would rip the woman away from the wall, **tearing off her breast**.

FACT 330 👉 **Use of the Spanish spider was rare** and generally reserved for women who were adulterous or self-aborted their unborn children.

FACT 331 👉 A humiliation device for meddlesome women or gossipers, the brank was a **metal head enclosure** that victims were forced to wear for hours, days, or sometimes months.

FACT 332 👉 **Some branks were adorned with spikes to pierce the skin** every time the wearer spoke, or with bells to let everyone know she was coming.

are you sh*tting me?

FACT 333 👈 Toe wedging dates back to Ancient Egypt but was also widely used in the Middle Ages. The torturer **placed a metal or wooden wedge between the victim's toe and toenail**, and slowly lifted the wedge to rip the nail from the nail bed. If the victim didn't confess, on to the next toe!

FACT 334 👈 Many toe-wedging victims ended up as amputees or contracted severe—and sometimes fatal—infections because **the wedges were rarely cleaned**.

FACT 335 👈 Victims of the **copper boot** had their feet locked into the device, which was then filled with water and boiled over a fire. Molten metal was sometimes used instead of water.

FACT 336 👈 Copper boots were **used mainly to extract confessions**, though victims would occasionally pass out or die before confessing.

FACT 337 👈 The street sweeper's daughter or scavenger's daughter was a **compression device** that forced the victim so tightly into a fetal or crouching position that it caused broken bones and spine dislocation.

FACT 338 👉 The street sweeper's daughter also **made victims' noses, ears, and even fingertips spray blood**.

FACT 339 👉 Though the street sweeper's daughter was used primarily for public humiliation, some victims were **left in the device for weeks** until they went mad or died.

9

Public Bathrooms

AT FIRST GLANCE, "PUBLIC bathrooms" looks like "pubic bathrooms," and that's not really a stretch, either. Every time you use a public toilet, you are basically sharing genital germs with every other person who has been in there since the place was last cleaned—which in some instances looks to be around 1974.

Here's my beef with public bathrooms: every time I go into one—which is as infrequently as I can—some 475-pound guy camped out in the end stall with the Sunday paper is absolutely destroying the place with his colon. I really hate having to hold my breath when I pee. It's not nearly as satisfying.

FACT 340 **One in five people have accidentally dropped a cell phone in the toilet.** No word on what percentage of them pull it out.

FACT 341 The stall closest to the door is likely to be **the cleanest and least-used seat** in a public restroom; the stall in the middle is usually the dirtiest.

FACT 342 Tech-savvy travelers can scope out the best public bathrooms in an area by **using mobile device apps to read how other users have rated a bathroom's cleanliness**. I never want to use public bathrooms enough to need that app.

FACT 343 👉 The dirtiest places in a public bathroom are typically **the sanitary napkin dispenser and the floor**. Toilet seats are actually among the cleaner spots in a public bathroom.

FACT 344 👉 Americans spend an average of **two weeks a year on the toilet**.

FACT 345 👉 The hole still found in the spine of every issue of the **Old Farmer's Almanac** is a carryover from the days when the magazine was typically hung on a hook in outhouses.

FACT 346 👉 **More homes in Japan have a washeretto**—a high-function toilet with multiple features—than a computer.

FACT 347 👉 Game company Sega has a new way to keep you occupied while you pee: they are **testing video games in public bathrooms** that are controlled by targeting your urine stream.

FACT 348   Medieval castle dwellers would do their business in a room called a garderobe, which was built to extend out beyond the rest of the castle so that **waste would fall outside the walls or into the moat**. Yeah! Fuck the neighbors!

FACT 349 **Ancient Rome's more than 140 public toilets were social hubs where friends would meet and chat while doing their potty business.**

FACT 350   In Singapore, you can be **fined up to $150 for failing to flush a public toilet**.

FACT 351   Some Singapore **elevators feature urine detectors** that will lock the doors shut and alert the police if someone tries to pee inside them.

are you sh*tting me?

FACT 352 👈 **Airplane bathrooms are among the dirtiest of all public bathrooms.** The small space makes it harder to wash your hands, and the flushing mechanism of the toilet sprays germs and fecal particles over the small area.

FACT 353 👈 Nine of ten baby-changing tables in UK public bathrooms were found to have **traces of cocaine on them**. Now there's a great idea: snort something off the same surface where you change poopy diapers.

FACT 354 👈 After its invention, **toilet paper wasn't immediately popular**. People were too ashamed to ask for it in drugstores. But they weren't embarrassed to wipe their asses with corncobs?

FACT 355 👈 In 1997, teen Melissa Drexler **gave birth in a school bathroom** during her prom, used the edge of a paper towel dispenser to cut the cord, then left the baby in a Dumpster and returned to the dance.

FACT 356 👉 The Pentagon was built with **twice as many bathrooms as necessary** because at the time it was constructed, Virginia law dictated that there be separate facilities for blacks and whites.

FACT 357 👉 Among the **germs we risk exposure to in public restrooms** are "streptococcus, staphylococcus, *E. coli* and shigella bacteria, hepatitis A virus, the common cold virus, and various sexually transmitted organisms."

FACT 358 👉 Because germs in feces are dispersed through the air when you flush the toilet, one expert recommends you **leave the stall right after flushing**. Says Philip Tierno, M.D., director of clinical microbiology and diagnostic immunology at New York University Medical Center and Mt. Sinai Medical Center, "The greatest aerosol dispersal occurs not during the initial moments of the flush, but rather once most of the water has already left the bowl."

FACT 359 👉 Due to organisms breeding in water, sinks tend to contain the **largest concentration** of germs in restrooms.

FACT 360 👉 Though 95 percent of people claim to wash their hands after using public restrooms, a study conducted by the American Society for Microbiology found that **only 67 percent actually do**.

FACT 361 👉 Philip Tierno, author of *The Secret Life of Germs*, says that **even people who do wash their hands might not be doing it right**. "Some individuals move their hands quickly under a flow of water for only a second or so, and they don't use soap. That's not going to do much good."

FACT 362 👉 Fecal germs can travel through **ten layers** of toilet paper.

10

Lies, Liars, and Frauds

"LIES, LIES, LIES, YEAH," the old 1980s song goes, "they're gonna get you!" So true. Lies and deception are tireless pursuers; just when you think you've gotten away with something, BAM! Busted!

What's funny is that *we know this*! Even as we're lying through our teeth or trying to pull a fast one on somebody, in the back of our minds we're saying, "I'll never get away with this." But do we stop? Nope.

Then, to top it all off, we have the nerve to be surprised when we get caught!

FACT 363 Thermographic cameras show that **your nose becomes warmer when you lie**.

FACT 364 Small lies told over text messages, such as "Can't talk, in a meeting," are called **"butler lies."**

FACT 365 **Unbroken eye contact** is not a sign of honesty, but a good clue that someone is lying.

FACT 366 Lie detection expert Dr. Paul Ekman claims that he and the researchers he trains can **spot a lie with 95 percent accuracy**.

FACT 367 People are more likely to lie when they are **in a hurry**.

FACT 368 A study at Notre Dame University found that **the more you lie, the less healthy you will be**. Test subjects who told more lies reported more mental and physical complaints than the non-lying group, including stress, sadness, headaches, and sore throats.

FACT 369 Research suggests that the average American tells about seven lies a week. OK—that's a lie. We tell about **eleven lies a week**, on average.

FACT 370 Eight percent of Americans have **lied on their résumés**.

FACT 371 People trust **bearded men** more than clean-shaven ones.

FACT 372 👉 **A person's dying words** are often admissible in court thanks to an old legal concept that a person would not lie with his dying breath.

FACT 373 👉 In an experiment intended to replicate a survival-of-the-fittest scenario, **robots learned to lie** to each other about the location of food resources in order to improve their own chances of survival.

FACT 374 👉 Rosie Ruiz cheated her way to first place in the 1980 **Boston Marathon** by running onto the course about a mile before the finish line.

FACT 375 👉 A reporter later claimed that Ruiz had also **faked her run** in the New York Marathon, which had qualified her for the Boston race, claiming Ruiz had ridden the subway for part of the New York race.

FACT 376 👉 Famous con artist Victor Lustig once **sold the Eiffel Tower** to a scrap dealer in Paris for $70,000, convincing the man he was a representative of the government, which was selling the monument.

FACT 377 👉 A few years after the execution of Russia's Czar Nicholas II and his family during the Bolshevik Revolution, a young woman came forward claiming to be the czar's daughter, the **grand duchess Anastasia**. The woman maintained her story until the day she died, but her claim was proved false when DNA tests showed no relation between her and the former royal family.

FACT 378 👉 In 1817, a woman speaking a strange tongue arrived in England, claiming to be Princess Caraboo from the island of Javasu. After gaining significant fame, she was exposed as **a cobbler's daughter** from Devonshire, not royalty and not from Javasu.

FACT 379 👉 **Internet scams** are among the top five industries in Nigeria.

FACT 380 👉 Many of the "walk" buttons in New York City do not actually trigger a walk light. Light changes are controlled by computers, and **the buttons are a placebo**. I don't care; I'm gonna keep pushing them ten or twelve times because it feels good.

FACT 381 In 1725, Professor Dr. Johann Beringer of the University of Würzburg thought he had made an incredible discovery when he found strange fossils with runes and shapes during an archaeological dig. His colleagues later admitted to planting the **fake stones** to trick Beringer.

FACT 382 Famous con man Frank Abagnale escaped from a Georgia prison by **convincing guards he was an undercover agent** from the U.S. Bureau of Prisons. The guards said they had known all along who he was and released him promptly.

FACT 383 Frank Abagnale eluded authorities a second time by **impersonating a government agent**. When his hotel was surrounded by the FBI, he walked out and claimed he was also FBI, then left the scene unhindered.

are you sh*tting me?

FACT 384 👉 German magazine *Stern* announced in 1983 that it had received **Adolf Hitler's personal diaries**. The diaries, which included mundane entries such as "Eva says I have bad breath," were authenticated by a handwriting expert but later exposed as a hoax.

FACT 385 👉 The medical study proposing a link between autism and vaccines was **exposed as fraudulent** in 2004, with the data cherry-picked, altered, and misrepresented. Investigators found that the doctor who published the study was on the payroll of a group that had filed a lawsuit against the manufacturers of the vaccine in question.

FACT 386 👉 In 1989, two scientists reported that they had discovered **cold fusion**, a solution to all the world's energy needs. When other scientists couldn't replicate their findings, the claim was exposed as a fraud.

FACT 387 👉 The Cardiff Giant hoax, one of the most famous in American history, began in 1869 when workers digging a well in Cardiff, New York, thought they discovered a **ten-foot-tall petrified man**. The "man" turned out to be a stone carving created and buried as a gag.

FACT 388 👉 George Hull, the man behind the Cardiff Giant hoax, did it to **mock local clergymen** who insisted that giants once walked the earth because the Bible said so.

FACT 389 👉 In 1912, an amateur archaeologist discovered the **Piltdown Man**, considered the earliest settler of England. Forty years later, the discovery was found to be a fake: the jaw of the skull was from an orangutan.

FACT 390 👉 Olympic gold medalist Stella Walsh was considered one of the fastest female athletes of her time—until her death, when she was discovered to **have a penis**.

FACT 391 👉 **After American Fred Lorz won the marathon at the 1904 Olympics well ahead of everyone else, it was discovered he had hitched a ride in a stranger's car for eleven miles** of the race. What, that's not allowed?

FACT 392 🖝 Bernie Madoff's massive **Ponzi scheme** netted $65 billion. After his conviction, Madoff's home and other property was sold to pay restitution to his victims.

FACT 393 🖝 The Securities and Exchange Commission was **tipped off repeatedly** about Bernie Madoff by a financial analyst who had figured out what Madoff was doing.

FACT 394 🖝 Monroe Beachy is called the **"Amish Bernie Madoff"** for stealing around $16.8 million from investors, most of them from Amish communities.

FACT 395 🖝 The Albanian Revolution of 1997 began as a protest over the collapse of a **government-reported pyramid scheme** that cost hundreds of thousands of citizens their life savings.

FACT 396 The Ponzi scheme is named for **Charles Ponzi**, a swindler who got rich using pyramid schemes and other illegal methods in 1920s Boston.

FACT 397 Lou Pearlman, creator of the boy band groups Backstreet Boys and 'N Sync, is currently in jail for **stealing $300 million from investors and banks** via a Ponzi scheme. He should've already been in jail for creating the Backstreet Boys and 'N Sync.

11

Birth Control

I HAVE ONE CHILD; that is enough. I love her, but I understand the desire to prevent pregnancy. But if you think people are serious about birth control now, wait until you read about some of the crazy crap they tried in ye olden tymes to avoid getting knocked up. I know they didn't have the Pill back then, but you have to wonder about anyone so desperate not to conceive that she would stuff her cooch with crocodile poop.

FACT 398 To prevent pregnancy, Indonesian Bataks insert bamboo or the **sharp part of a leaf** into a woman's vagina.

FACT 399 Early condoms were made of **fish bladders**, animal intestines, and linen soaked with chemicals to prevent disease.

FACT 400 **The "pull-out" birth control method** has been around since the Old Testament, when Onan "spills his seed on the ground" before getting busy with his new wife so that she wouldn't become pregnant.

FACT 401 Greek physician Soranus suggested that women could avoid pregnancy by **squatting and forcing themselves to sneeze after coitus**. No word on what he recommended for a sore anus.

FACT 402 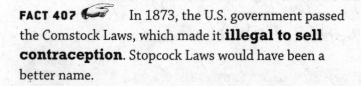 Women have historically used many different materials as **pessaries** (cervix blockers), ranging from grass to rice tissue paper to sea sponges.

FACT 403 Egyptian women used **crocodile dung** as a spermicide.

FACT 404 The German word for the birth control pill is, conveniently, **antibabypille**.

FACT 405 **Baboons eat plums** as a natural form of birth control: the fruit has chemicals that work similar to progesterone, one of the active ingredients in birth control pills.

FACT 406 In ancient Greece an herb called **silphion** became so popular as a natural oral contraceptive that the plant was extinct by 100 C.E.

FACT 407 In 1873, the U.S. government passed the Comstock Laws, which made it **illegal to sell contraception**. Stopcock Laws would have been a better name.

FACT 408 👉 In the early twentieth century, *feminine hygiene products* was a widely used euphemism for **contraception**.

FACT 409 👉 The first **family planning clinic** was opened in 1916 but was shut down ten days later—due to poor planning.

FACT 410 👉 **Lysol was commonly used as contraception** before modern birth control was developed. Women suffered burns, and the method did not prevent pregnancy.

FACT 411 👉 Early Egyptians used tampons made of **wool dipped in honey and acacia** to prevent pregnancy. Fermented acacia contains an ingredient used in modern spermicides.

FACT 412  Famous lover Casanova reported that women used **lemon halves** as cervical caps to prevent pregnancy.

FACT 413 Women in the Middle Ages were advised to **use talismans** to ward off pregnancy; one suggestion was to hang weasel testicles from their thighs.

FACT 414 Hippocrates suggested that women eat the **seeds of the wild carrot** (also called Queen Anne's lace) to prevent pregnancy. Modern studies suggest this is actually an effective contraceptive.

FACT 415 In the Greek myth of Persephone, the young goddess is **forced to live in the underworld** for half a year after eating pomegranate seeds; the seeds were also used as a contraceptive in ancient Greece.

FACT 416 👉 Early Japanese condoms were **made of turtle shell** and covered only the glans (head) of the penis. That doesn't sound painful at all.

FACT 417 👉 Condoms were first associated with prostitutes, and people gave them **euphemistic nicknames**: the English called them French letters, and the French called them *capotes anglaises* (British overcoats).

12

Mental Monarchs

ABSOLUTE POWER CORRUPTS ABSOLUTELY. Especially if you were an inbred nut job in the first place. That said, it wouldn't be horrible to have unlimited money, unlimited power, and unlimited freedom to do whatever you wanted, whenever you wanted, and to whomever you wanted to do it. Sure, sooner or later your subjects would get tired of your crap and kill you, but you would have some seriously good times before it all went south.

FACT 418  Roman Emperor Gaius Caesar (37–41), also known as **Caligula**, or "Little Boot," was a cruel and mercurial leader who found torture and executions entertaining.

FACT 419 Caligula often forced parents to **watch their sons being killed**.

FACT 420 As a teenager, Caligula is believed to have committed **incest** with his sister Drusilla.

FACT 421 Caligula was assassinated in 41 C.E. by a group of his closest advisers, who **stabbed him thirty times**. His wife and daughter were also murdered.

FACT 422 So roundly hated was Caligula that after his death, the senate ordered **the destruction of all statues of him**.

FACT 423  Roman Emperor **Nero** (54–68) was a sadistic, sexually depraved lunatic who took his mother as a lover, then had her killed when she tried to control him.

FACT 424 Later in his reign, the emperor was unforgiving of perceived disloyalty or criticism. He had an army commander **executed for speaking against him** at a party.

FACT 425 Nero tried to **strangle his first wife**, Octavia, then had her executed after she divorced him.

FACT 426 Two weeks after divorcing Octavia, **Nero married Poppaea Sabina**, the widow of a Roman knight whom Nero had ordered to be killed.

FACT 427 During a quarrel with a pregnant Poppaea, **Nero kicked her to death**.

FACT 428 When Roman emperor Claudius's daughter Antonia refused to become Nero's next wife, she was **charged with rebellion and executed**.

FACT 429   One of Nero's "wives" was an adolescent boy whom the emperor had ordered to be **castrated**.

FACT 430 Many Romans suspected that **Nero started the great fire of Rome** in 64 C.E. to make room for a new villa he was planning to build. The emperor blamed the Christians, which became a starting point for their persecution and torture in Rome.

FACT 431 Nero wasn't all bad: he **banished mimes** in Rome.

FACT 432 Ancient historian John of Ephesus recounts that Emperor Justin II of Byzantine (who ruled from 565 to 574) **heard voices in his head** and, to escape them, would scream and hide under his bed or order his servants to play organ music throughout the palace.

FACT 433 The only thing that abated Justin's crazy behavior was a **makeshift throne on wheels** built by his servants, who would push the emperor up and down palace halls.

FACT 434 👉 King Charles VI of France (1368–1422) had **iron rods inserted into his clothing** because he was convinced he was made of glass and would break.

- -

FACT 435 👉 In 1392, Charles **killed four of his own men** during a manic episode after a page startled him by dropping a lance. At least he didn't overreact.

- -

FACT 436 👉 **Charles would go months without bathing** and often prowled the corridors of his palace, howling like a wild animal.

- -

FACT 437 👉 After her husband died in 1506, Queen Juana of Spain (a.k.a. Joanna of Castille) was so heartbroken that **she kept his coffin with her** at all times so she could gaze at his rotting remains.

FACT 438 👉   A new theory suggests that a condition called **McLeod syndrome** could have been responsible for the mental and physical deterioration of King Henry VIII (who ruled from 1509 to 1547) later in his life. Older men are at risk from this disease, which has symptoms that include heart disease, movement disorders, and major psychological conditions such as paranoia and dementia.

FACT 439 👉   The same theory suggests that Henry VIII had **a rare blood type called Kell positive**, which could have contributed to the frequent miscarriages of his many wives.

FACT 440 👉   Born in 1530, Czar Ivan IV, a.k.a. Ivan the Terrible, was a sensitive and intelligent boy who **tortured small animals** for sport. OK, maybe not so sensitive.

FACT 441 👉   Ivan was an **unpopular leader** who seized private lands to give to his supporters and caused major disruptions in the Russian economy and culture.

FACT 442 👉 Ivan created the Oprichniki, **the first official secret Russian police force**. Dressed in black astride black horses, the Oprichniki existed more to crush dissent than to keep the peace.

FACT 443 👉 After the death of his first wife in 1560, **Ivan became even more brutal**, destroying the major families of nobility in the region whom he had long suspected of being involved in his mother's murder.

FACT 444 👉 Ivan's other misdeeds included **beating his pregnant daughter-in-law** badly enough to cause a miscarriage; murdering his son; and blinding the architect of St. Basil's Cathedral.

FACT 445 👉 Laughing, smiling, or whispering within earshot of the **slightly paranoid** King Erik XIV of Sweden (who ruled from 1560 to 1568) often earned people a charge of treason and a death sentence.

FACT 446 👉 King Erik was certain for a time that **he was his own brother**. In 1568, his real brother replaced him as king after advisers deemed Erik too unstable to rule.

FACT 447 👉 Erik was fed **poisoned pea soup** and killed in 1577.

FACT 448 👉 Known for his "vacant gaze," Czar Fyodor I of Russia (who ruled from 1584 to 1598), son of Ivan the Terrible, left **ruling the kingdom** up to his brother-in-law, Boris Godunov. Instead, he wandered throughout the country, determined to ring all of the church bells in Russia.

FACT 449 👉 In 1626, German princess Maria Eleonora of Brandenburg, desperate to give her husband a male heir, **seemed to lose her mind** after the birth of a daughter instead. Calling the child a "monster," Maria tried to kill the baby on many occasions, often "accidentally" dropping her or shoving her down the stairs.

FACT 450 👉 One of the most notorious of the Ottoman sultans, Ibrahim I (who ruled from 1640 to 1648) was known as **Ibrahim the Mad** due to his frequent nervous attacks and general mental instability.

FACT 451 👉 In one fit of madness, Ibrahim had **his entire harem of 280 concubines drowned** in the Bosphorus. Sometimes you just have to start fresh, you know?

are you sh*tting me?

FACT 452 Midway through his reign (1760–1820), King George III began to show signs of insanity, including **acute agitation, temper outbursts, and profane verbal tirades** that went on for hours until the king would foam at the mouth. Or, as it's called at my house, "homework time."

FACT 453 When George became too combative, he was **put in a straitjacket** or tied to his bed.

FACT 454 King George, says author Michael Farquhar, "**gave orders to people who did not exist**. He composed letters to foreign courts on imaginary causes, and lavished honors on all who approached him, even the lowliest servant."

FACT 455 During one dinner, **George suddenly attacked his eldest son**, pulling him out of his chair and throwing him against the wall.

FACT 456 According to Michael Farquhar, "Historians now believe that King George's strange behavior was **caused by a rare hereditary blood disorder** called porphyria. Symptoms of the condition include many exhibited by George, such as severe abdominal pain, weakness of limbs, discolored urine, rambling speech, hallucinations, hysteria, paranoia, and schizophrenia."

FACT 457 King Christian VII of Denmark (who ruled from 1766 to 1808) was known for **throwing food at dinner guests** and would sometimes slap people in the face in the middle of a conversation for no reason.

FACT 458 Christian developed such a **chronic masturbation habit** that court physicians worried it would stunt his growth or render him infertile.

FACT 459 Queen Maria I of Portugal (who ruled from 1777 to 1816) had **a religious fanaticism** that led her to believe she was going to hell. She also claimed to have seen her deceased father's burnt corpse being tortured by demons.

FACT 460 Princess Alexandra Amelie of Bavaria (1826–1875) believed she had swallowed a glass piano as a child. She also had an **obsession with cleanliness** and would wear only white clothing.

FACT 461 Ferdinand I of Austria (who ruled from 1835 to 1848) reportedly spoke only one sentence in his life: **"I am the Emperor, and I want dumplings."** As a result of inbreeding—his parents were double first cousins—Ferdinand was epileptic, encephalitic, and practically mute.

FACT 462 After his cabinet accused him of insanity, Bavaria's "Märchenkönig" (fairy-tale king) Ludwig II (who ruled from 1864 to 1886) was placed in custody. The following day, Ludwig disappeared. Hours later, his lifeless body was **found floating in a lake**. The circumstances of his death remain a mystery to this day.

FACT 463 Engaged but never married, Ludwig's diary entries suggest that he **struggled with his sexual orientation** throughout his adult life.

FACT 464 👉 Advisers to King Otto of Bavaria (who ruled from 1886 to 1913) included **ghosts in his dresser drawers**, who Otto claimed told him to have a peasant shot every day.

FACT 465 👉 The last ruling king of Egypt, Farouk (who ruled from 1936 to 1952), indulged in excessive partying and gambling. He reportedly **drank thirty bottles of soda a day** and ate caviar from the can.

FACT 466 👉 Farouk was a **kleptomaniac** who once stole a watch from Winston Churchill.

FACT 467 👉 After having nightmares about lions attacking him, King Farouk **shot all the lions** at the Cairo zoo.

FACT 468 👉 Found among Farouk's treasures after he was overthrown in 1952 was **the world's largest collection of porn**.

 are you sh*tting me?

13

Creepy Crawlies

I LIVE IN THE South, where cockroaches are so common, they should be a state bird, especially those flying ones that people euphemistically call "Crescent bugs." Crescent bug, my ass: that's a roach! I don't mind most creepy crawlies, but I hate me some roaches.

That said, there is one thing I do like about roaches: the crunching sound they make when I crush them with my foot. It's like they are made of tiny brittle twigs, each one snapping as I press down harder with my shoe. *Snap* *Crackle* *Pop*

It's not that I'm cruel. Most bugs in my house get taken outside to live another day. But not cockroaches. They are the exception. If you are a cockroach and you come into my home, you will die. Slowly and painfully. And loudly.

You are warned.

FACT 469 The **scabies mite** is a tiny eight-legged insect that can live under our skin. After mating, the female mite burrows into the top skin layer and lays several eggs a day.

FACT 470 The scabies mite's preferred burrowing locations are the **hands, wrist, armpits, and genitals**.

FACT 471 Scabies' **eggs and poop trigger an allergic reaction** in our skin, causing severe itching.

FACT 472 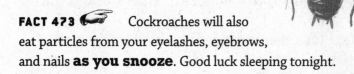 A cockroach will eat almost anything, including **dead skin and dirty clothes**.

FACT 473 Cockroaches will also eat particles from your eyelashes, eyebrows, and nails **as you snooze**. Good luck sleeping tonight.

FACT 474 Debris from cockroach skins, dead bodies, and droppings **can cause allergies** in people, especially children and those with existing allergy issues.

FACT 475 Cockroaches can be difficult to find in your home because **they are nocturnal** and adept at hiding. Many over-the-counter insecticides also prove ineffective on their eggs.

FACT 476 A cockroach **can live two weeks without water** and almost a month without food. Just like Kate Moss.

FACT 477 **Bedbugs bite mostly during the night.** Their mouths are specially adapted for piercing skin and sucking blood.

FACT 478 👉 **Bedbug bites** are hard to detect because the insects inject anti-inflammatory agents that make you less likely to feel irritation or get a sore. They are thoughtful insects.

FACT 479 👉 The toxins produced by mold **are invisible and can penetrate food**. Even if you remove visible mold from foods, toxins can remain and cause illness if eaten.

FACT 480 👉 Insects and spiders have been known to **take up residence in the human ear**. Your ear suddenly itches, doesn't it? Mine does.

FACT 481 👉 Itching and strange noises in her ear led a woman in Cardiff, Wales, to seek medical treatment in 2003. Doctors found a **spider living in her ear canal**.

are you sh*tting me?

FACT 482 In 1997, a man suffering from severe ear pain visited a doctor, who found the man's **ear canal filled with maggots**. The doctor suspected that a fly had gotten into the man's ear as he slept and lain eggs.

FACT 483 The bites of two insects, the blackfly and the buffalo gnat, can introduce a parasitic worm larvae into the human body that can be carried through the bloodstream and **take up residence in your eyes**. That's right: worms in your eyes.

FACT 484 These parasitic worms can cause **inflammation, bleeding, and blindness**.

FACT 485 Known as the **"brain-eating amoeba,"** *Naegleria fowleri* is a microscopic organism that can cause primary amebic meningoencephalitis (PAM), a rare and fatal disease of the central nervous system.

FACT 486 The *Naegleria* amoeba is found **all over the world** in warm stagnant bodies of fresh water such as lakes, rivers, hot springs, and unchlorinated swimming pools.

FACT 487  The amoeba enters the body through the nose, then climbs **along nerve fibers** through the skull and into the brain.

FACT 488  *Naegleria* amoebas **love the warmth of the brain** and will multiply in the millions until the victim drops dead, usually within three to seven days of infestation.

FACT 489  There have been roughly **two hundred recorded cases** of *Naegleria* infection worldwide in the last four years. Children are thought to be more at risk because of weaker immune systems.

FACT 490  Rats tend to **live in subterranean sewers**, which allows them to take advantage of the food waste that accumulates there. They have been known to follow the waste trail in toilets or sinks into homes.

FACT 491 🖝 Rat has become a common meal in a number of Asian countries—vendors in Thailand sell them both raw and roasted. **Barbecued rat**, which can be found in Vietnam and Cambodia, is said to have a stringier consistency than chicken.

FACT 492 🖝 **Rats are known to eat their young** in certain situations. Scientists think mother rats feed on their weaker young to save the energy they'd otherwise have to spend caring for the runts.

FACT 493 🖝 A 2008 study found that **cannibalism of infant rats** occurred more frequently when the rodents were kept in cleaner cages. Scientists believe that the rats struggled to detect family members' natural scents because of the cleaner environment.

FACT 494 🖝 A rat's teeth are extremely sharp. **A rat bite can penetrate a toenail.**

FACT 495 🖝 **Your food may contain rat feces.** The U.S. Food and Drug Administration allows a small amount of droppings to be present in commercial food products because rats find their way into the products so frequently.

FACT 496 Indonesia's **Mallomys rat** is five times bigger than the average rat and weighs in at roughly six pounds.

FACT 497 Rats have indiscriminate mating habits, **often copulating with siblings or parents**. As a result, rats are the largest single group of mammals in the animal kingdom.

Colossal Blunders

IDON'T YOU LOVE THIS word that politicians like to use nowadays: *misspoke*? As if any idiotic statement or flat-out lie can be wiped away by saying, "Oops, I misspoke."

We should apply the same logic to other screw-ups, especially big ones. Did you run your passenger ship into an iceberg and kill thousands of people? Just say you *misboated*. It's much less severe, isn't it? If you accidentally carve the wrong word into a stone monument meant to last for eternity, simply say you *mischiseled*. See how easy this is?

By the way, if you find any errors in this book, forgive me: I miswrote.

FACT 498 👉 All of the original footage from **America's first moon landing** was permanently lost in the 1980s when other video was recorded over it.

FACT 499 👉 In 2007, a New Jersey cable company inadvertently broadcast **hard-core porn** during children's programming. Instead of the regularly scheduled show, *Handy Manny*, the kids saw the movie *Mandy Gives a Handy*.

FACT 500 👉 When Norway fired a research rocket toward Russia in 1997, Norwegian **officials forgot to alert** the Russian government, nearly causing a retaliatory strike from that country.

FACT 501 In 1981, 114 people were killed when **skywalks collapsed** at the Hyatt Regency hotel in Kansas City, Missouri. The accident was attributed to a last-minute design change that left one skywalk hanging from another instead of both being bolted to the ceiling.

FACT 502 The Lincoln Memorial **originally had a typo**: the word *future* was spelled "euture." The correction is still visible on the statue. Oh well, at least it wasn't carved in stone.

FACT 503 In 1987, an observant college student found **a mistake in Isaac Newton's published mathematics work** that had been overlooked by scholars for three hundred years.

FACT 504 In 1999, NASA's Mars Climate Orbiter **got too close to the red planet** and burned up because of a simple error: one group working on the project was using imperial units while the other used metric.

FACT 505 The steamship *Eastland* rolled over on its side in the Chicago River in 1915, killing 844 people in twenty feet of water. The accident was blamed on **the weight of the lifeboats** that were added after the *Titanic* disaster.

FACT 506 In 1913, a man falsely yelled "Fire!" at a crowded Christmas Eve party in Calumet, Michigan, setting off **a stampede that killed seventy-four people**, most of them children.

FACT 507 In 1972, **a conservation group dumped millions of tires** in the ocean off of Fort Lauderdale, Florida, to help clear landfills and buffer dying coral reefs, but the debris has destroyed more marine life than it has saved.

FACT 508 There is a growing population of **radioactive wild boar** in the area around the former Chernobyl Nuclear Power Plant.

FACT 509 🖐️ A Japanese commercial 727 crashed in 1971 after being struck by a **student pilot**. All 162 people aboard the commercial jet died, but the flight student parachuted to safety.

FACT 510 🖐️ More than seven thousand people die every year due to their **doctors' bad handwriting**.

FACT 511 🖐️ In 1992, underground explosions rocked the city of Guadalajara, Mexico, damaging hundreds of buildings and killing more than two hundred people. The explosions were **caused by a gas leak** that officials had been warned about hours before but had ignored.

FACT 512 🖐️ During World War I, two ships struck each other in port at Halifax, Nova Scotia, after a brief dispute over right of way. One ship was carrying munitions and blew up, creating the **largest man-made explosion in history**; it killed fifteen hundred people and caused a tsunami.

FACT 513   Only **four months after it was erected** in 1940, the Tacoma Narrows Bridge in Washington collapsed in a windstorm.

are you sh*tting me?

15

Parenting
You're Doing It Wrong

HAVE YOU EVER FELT like the world's worst parent? Of course you have. Most parents have those days, including me. But get ready to feel a lot better about yourself, because you and I have nothing on the nitwits you'll read about in this chapter. Did you ever let your toddler fire a submachine gun at police while driving a car with a dead body in the trunk? No? Then you're doing just fine as a parent.

FACT 514 Jessica Black of Craigsville, Virginia, let her seven-year-old **dress as a member of the Ku Klux Klan** for Halloween in 2013. She defended the choice by claiming that the Klan raises money for St. Jude Children's Research Hospital.

FACT 515 After she allowed her nine-year-old son and his five-year-old playmate to **go on a joy ride** in her car to "take out the trash," Michigan mom Leah Michele Jaglowski was arrested for contributing to the delinquency of a minor.

FACT 516 In October 2013, Shambreya Barfield and Trevell Washington caused a thirty-person brawl in front of dozens of children at a Chuck E. Cheese's in Chicago after **arguing over prize tickets**. Both were arrested and charged with battery.

FACT 517 👉 A Redmond, Washington, father was charged with attempted murder in September 2013 after **injecting his four-year-old son with heroin**. The boy, who also had codeine, ketamine, and morphine in his system, miraculously lived.

FACT 518 👉 An eleven-year-old boy in Las Vegas, Nevada, suffered burns on 40 percent of his body after his mother got **behind on her minivan payments** in September 2013 and instructed the child to douse the car with gasoline and set it on fire.

FACT 519 👉 When a woman in Yuzhou, China, was stopped for recklessly operating her moped in September 2013, police found out why: she was **breast-feeding her child while driving**. Her driving was probably fine until the baby started biting.

FACT 520 👉 In December 2013, sixteen-year-old Ethan Couch struck and killed four pedestrians while drunk driving. Incredibly, Couch was sentenced only to probation after his defense attorneys argued that he **suffered from "affluenza,"** meaning his wealthy parents never set limits for him.

FACT 521 A Missouri woman faced a criminal charge in December 2013 after **snapping a topless photo of herself and her fourteen-year-old daughter** in a hot tub. Police were made aware of the photo after it began circulating at a pair of local high schools.

FACT 522 In January 2012, a Florida mother was arrested for child abuse and contributing to the delinquency of a minor after police saw a Facebook video of the woman **encouraging her teenage daughter during an after-school fight** instead of stopping the altercation.

FACT 523 Another Florida mother was busted for felony child abuse in August 2013 after **biting her sixteen-year-old daughter's "right breast in the nipple area"** during a fight over Social Security benefits for the daughter's newborn baby.

FACT 524 👉 In March 2014, a Maryland grandmother was arrested while **trying to steal a teacher's wallet** as she visited her grandchild's elementary school for a morning assembly. Because teachers make so much money.

FACT 525 👉 Police were summoned to a 2013 Easter egg hunt at Woodland Park Zoo in Seattle when one woman reportedly "**pushed a child aside** as her own child scrambled toward some brightly colored eggs." The two mothers began fighting, leaving one woman with a bloody nose.

FACT 526 👉 A new father in China filed for divorce in 2012 after his wife gave birth to what he considered to be **an ugly child**. He later sued his ex for misrepresenting her contribution to the gene pool when he found out she'd had extensive plastic surgery. A judge ruled in the man's favor and awarded him $120,000 in damages.

FACT 527 👉 An Arizona mother was arrested in 2013 after **giving beer to her two-year-old son** at a pizza parlor. After the toddler fell out of his high chair, a witness called police to report the incident.

FACT 528 👉 A Sacramento, California, grandmother was arrested for felony child endangerment in October 2013 after **trying to give her four-year-old granddaughter away to a stranger**. The woman had taken the child to a grassy area near a busy intersection and drunk vodka until she passed out, prompting the stranger to stop and offer assistance.

FACT 529 👉 An Oklahoma woman was arrested in March 2013 for **trying to sell her children on Facebook**. The mother offered her two kids, ages two and ten months, to another woman for cash, which she said she needed to bail her boyfriend out of jail.

FACT 530 👉 In 2012, a Wisconsin father of nine was given an unusual edict by a judge: **stop having kids**. The order was a condition of the man's parole after he was arrested for falling $90,000 behind on child support and related payments to the six women who bore his children.

16

Amusement Park Accidents

WARNING: THIS CHAPTER MIGHT make you never want to get on an amusement park ride again. If this were ten to fifteen years ago when I still liked amusement park rides, I wouldn't have tackled this subject. But now that I'm older, and suddenly and inexplicably unable to enjoy the same rides I used to love without barfing, there's nothing left to ruin for me. So I will ruin it for you instead. Call me selfish, but come on, did you really think that giant wood-and-metal rides operated by pimply-faced teens or inbred carny types were safe?

FACT 531 👉 **An average of forty-four hundred kids a year** are hurt on rides at carnivals and amusement parks, according to a twenty-year study of injury data from nearly a hundred nationally representative hospitals.

FACT 532 👉 Almost **seventy kids a year** sustain amusement park injuries serious enough to require hospitalization.

FACT 533 👉 Half of all amusement park accidents involve children **age thirteen and younger**.

FACT 534 👉 Between May and September each year—peak season for amusement parks—**approximately twenty children are hurt on park rides each day**, or one every two hours.

FACT 535 👉 Records show that **fifty-two ride-related deaths** occurred between 1990 and 2004.

are you sh*tting me?

FACT 536 👉 Data from the U.S. Consumer Product Safety Commission (CPSC) suggests that the rides at mobile carnivals and fairs have a **better safety record** than those at the big fixed-site parks because the former are subject to federal oversight while the latter are not.

FACT 537 👉 Records between 1987 and 2004 reveal only **thirteen mobile ride–related fatalities**, but forty-six fatalities associated with rides at fixed-site parks.

FACT 538 👉 **In 1981, the U.S. Congress stripped the CPSC of its authority to regulate rides at fixed-site parks** like Six Flags and Disneyland, determining that fixed-site amusement rides were sufficiently monitored by experts employed by the parks themselves. Right. Experts like my sixteen-year-old booger-eating nephew. I feel so much safer now.

FACT 539 Six states have no laws requiring state government oversight of park rides: Alabama, Mississippi, Nevada, South Dakota, Utah, and Wyoming. One of those, Wyoming, has no amusement parks.

FACT 540 On August 22, 1999, a twelve-year-old boy was killed after **plummeting two hundred feet** from the Drop Zone Stunt Tower at the Great America park in Santa Clara, California.

FACT 541 The next day, a twenty-year-old man **fell to his death** after partially removing a safety harness on the Shockwave roller coaster at Kings Dominion park in Virginia. Too bad they don't make a stupidity harness.

FACT 542 An Arkansas **woman drowned** in March 1999 when her raft capsized on the Roaring Rapids ride at Six Flags Over Texas. Ten other riders were injured.

FACT 543 In 2004, **an overweight man with cerebral palsy was killed** after being thrown from the Ride of Steel coaster at Six Flags New England in Springfield, Massachusetts.

are you sh*tting me?

FACT 544 👉 In June 1999, a Brooklyn teenager died on Coney Island's Super Himalaya after **her car decoupled** and she was thrown from the ride.

FACT 545 👉 In September 2013, thirteen people were injured at a carnival in Norwalk, Connecticut, when **a swing ride stopped suddenly**, causing suspended riders to crash into each other and the ride's center support column.

FACT 546 👉 In 2000, a four-year-old boy fell out of the Roger Rabbit's Car Toon Spin ride at Disneyland and was **run over by the car behind him**. The child suffered permanent brain damage and died in 2009 at age thirteen.

FACT 547 👉 In 1995, a woman filed suit against Disney, claiming she suffered a brain hemorrhage due to **"violent shaking, jolting, and jouncing"** on the Indiana Jones Adventure ride at Disneyland. Her lawyer obtained Disney records indicating scores of injuries on the same ride.

FACT 548 👉 Rosy Esparza, fifty-two, died on July 19, 2013, after being "apparently ejected" and **falling seventy-five feet** from the Texas Giant roller coaster at Six Flags Over Texas.

FACT 549 Esparza's family filed a wrongful death lawsuit against Six Flags on September 10, 2013, claiming that the park "should have known the dangers of putting patrons on coasters with **only lap bars** and no seat belts or harnesses."

FACT 550 The Esparza suit also asserts that, following the accident, inspections performed showed that "various parts of the security systems on the ride were experiencing **inconsistencies and intermittent failures.**" *Ya think?!*

FACT 551 In 2007, a thirteen-year-old girl had **both her feet severed** on the Superman Tower of Power at Six Flags Kentucky Kingdom when the ride's cabling snapped and tore through her legs.

FACT 552 👉 In 2011, a double-amputee Iraq war veteran **fell to his death** from the Darien Lake Theme Park's Ride of Steel roller coaster in Genesee County, New York.

FACT 553 👉 In April 2005, a teenager and her eleven-year-old cousin were **trapped nine hundred feet above the Las Vegas strip** for more than an hour when the Insanity ride suddenly shut down due to high winds.

FACT 554 👉 **A four-year-old boy died** in 2005 after passing out on Mission: Space, a turbulent motion-simulator ride at Walt Disney World's Epcot Future World in Orlando, Florida.

FACT 555 👉 In April 2006, a forty-nine-year-old woman also **became ill after riding Mission: Space**, and died the following day.

FACT 556 👉 A mother and her eight-year-old daughter were killed in August 1999 on the Wild Wonder coaster on the Ocean City, New Jersey, boardwalk after **a malfunction sent their car hurtling backward down a hill**, ejecting them.

FACT 557 The ride's emergency safety mechanism, an anti-rollback device similar to an **emergency brake**, failed to prevent the accident.

FACT 558 Two girls were killed and seven people were injured at International Park in Rosario, Argentina, when **a gondola detached from a Ferris wheel** and plummeted eighty feet to the ground.

FACT 559 Witnesses said that **the car fell from the highest point of the Ferris wheel** and struck the two girls on the ground, killing them.

FACT 560 A grandmother was killed at Six Flags New Orleans in July 2003, when **the Joker's Jukebox ride suddenly started** as she was strapping in her grandson, striking her in the head.

FACT 561 A stalled swing ride at Carowinds theme park in North Carolina left sixty-four passengers **hanging hundreds of feet above the ground** for over an hour in July 2013. The ride had stalled the previous year as well, when it left twenty-five riders trapped in the air for almost three hours.

FACT 562 🗨 A similar ride at Knott's Berry Farm in California stalled twice in September 2013, **stranding passengers in the air** for a combined seven hours.

FACT 563 🗨 After the Fujin Raijin II roller coaster at Expoland near Osaka, Japan, derailed in 2007, inspectors discovered that the coaster's axles were fifteen years old. **The accident injured nineteen people and killed one**, making it Japan's worst amusement park disaster to date.

FACT 564   Seven people were injured at Cedar Point theme park in Ohio in July 2013, when a boat on the Shoot the Rapids ride **slid backward down an incline and flipped over**.

FACT 565   At a Bellaire, Ohio, carnival in June 2013, **an eight-year-old boy was electrocuted** and hospitalized in critical condition when a live wire came loose and made contact with a metal ride railing on which he was leaning.

FACT 566   A six-year-old girl suffered collapsed lungs, a broken rib, and a broken arm after she became **pinned between a boat and boarding dock** at the It's a Small World ride at Walt Disney World in 1994. She probably jumped out of the boat early to get away from that god-awful song.

FACT 567   No heart defibrillators were available in the area when a forty-four-year-old man suffered a **fatal heart attack** on Disney World's Expedition Everest roller coaster in 2007.

are you sh*tting me?

FACT 568 Disney World's only **fatal monorail accident** occurred in 2009, when a track change malfunction caused two monorails to collide, killing one twenty-one-year-old driver.

FACT 569 A woman visiting Knott's Berry Farm in California in 2001 died when **she fell more than a hundred feet from the Perilous Plunge water ride**. Authorities said she "somehow got out . . . or came out of the ride" and landed in a body of water at the base of the attraction.

FACT 570 In 1978, at California's Six Flags Magic Mountain, **a gondola plunged** from its cable fifty feet to the ground, killing a man inside the car and injuring his wife. The man was reportedly rocking the car before it fell.

FACT 571 When the Demon coaster at Six Flags Great America in Illinois malfunctioned in April 1998, twenty-three people were stuck upside down for **nearly three hours**.

FACT 572 🖝 At the Battersea Park Fun Fair in England in 1972, a cable snapped on the Big Dipper coaster, **causing a chain of cars to roll backward down a hill**. Five children were killed and thirteen others were injured in one of the worst amusement park accidents in history.

FACT 573 🖝 A six-year-old boy died on the Puff the Little Fire Dragon ride at Utah's Lagoon Amusement Park in 1989 when **he slipped out of his safety restraint**, fell from the ride, and was struck by another car.

FACT 574 🖝 An eight-year-old girl lost part of her scalp at the now-defunct Bonkers 19 amusement park in Massachusetts when **her hair became tangled in the motor** behind her seat on the Mini Himalaya ride. Bonkers 19, scalp 0.

FACT 575 🖝 At Kings Island amusement park near Cincinnati, Ohio, a woman **fell to her death** from the Flight Commander ride on June 11, 1991. In an unrelated incident on the same day, two men were electrocuted in a pond inside the park.

are you sh*tting me?

Isolated Places

I DON'T MIND ISOLATION, but then I'm old and crusty and I talk to myself. Normal people don't like being separated from others for very long. That's why horror movies are often about someone trapped in an isolated place and why unruly prison inmates are tossed into solitary confinement.

Like it or not, we need other people. If you don't believe me, take a sabbatical and move to one of the places listed in this chapter for a year or so; see how that goes. Don't forget to send me a postcard. That is, if the place even has mail service. Or paper.

FACT 576 The Japanese island of Okunoshima, also called "Rabbit Island" after the many furry inhabitants who live there, was once home to **Japan's poison gas factories**. The rabbits are descendants of ones used for chemical testing during World War II.

FACT 577 The town of Centralia, Pennsylvania, has been abandoned since the 1980s due to **massive coal mine fires** that have burned steadily since 1962, producing gas leaks, dangerous temperatures, and giant sinkholes.

FACT 578 The underground fires at Centralia still have **enough fuel to burn for another 250 years**.

FACT 579   North Sentinel Island in the Indian Ocean is home to the Sentinelese, **the last known Stone Age tribe on earth**. The tribe has had little contact with the outside world, and they are hostile to outsiders. North Sentinel sounds a lot like Maine.

FACT 580   In 2006, the Sentinelese **killed two fishermen** whose boat drifted onto their shores and fired arrows at the helicopter sent to retrieve the bodies.

FACT 581   Reaching Belize's remote cave Actun Tunichil Muknal requires travelers to **walk for an hour through the jungle** before swimming and wading another kilometer up the cave river. Inside the cave are skeletons of ritual sacrifices made by the Maya to their gods more than a thousand years ago.

FACT 582   Some of those sacrificed in Actun Tunichil Muknal were children, including the **skeleton of a teenage girl** known as the Crystal Maiden because her calcified bones sparkle in the light.

FACT 583 🖝 Jazirat al Maqlab, or Telegraph Island, between the Persian Gulf and the Gulf of Oman, was a telegraph outpost used between 1864 and 1869 to facilitate communications between England and India. The location was so remote and desolate that it reportedly drove those stationed there to **lose their minds**.

FACT 584 🖝 **The world's farthest point from sea**, located more than 1,553 miles (2,500 kilometers) from any ocean, is the Eurasian Pole of Inaccessibility in northern China.

FACT 585 🖝 At 1,553 miles (2,500 kilometers) from any land mass, Point Nemo in the South Pacific is **the world's farthest point from land**.

FACT 586 🖝 The Southern Pole of Inaccessibility is the point in Antarctica that is farthest from the Southern Ocean—and thus **the most difficult to reach**. Those who do reach the station will find only a bust of Vladimir Lenin atop a research station buried under snow.

FACT 587 🖝 Growing in the middle of the Sahara Desert with **no other trees** within 250 miles, Niger's Tree of Ténéré was considered the most isolated tree in the world until a truck struck and killed it in 1973.

 are you sh*tting me?

FACT 588 The Old Forge pub in Scotland holds the Guinness World Record for **the most remote bar in Britain**. To reach it you'll need to walk twelve miles over land, though we recommend taking a boat, as the water route is much quicker.

FACT 589 **The most isolated inhabited island in the world is Tristan da Cunha**, an active volcano located in the middle of the south Atlantic Ocean 1,242 miles (2,000 kilometers) from the nearest land. Tristan da Cunha is Portuguese for "Where the fuck are we?!"

FACT 590 Tristan da Cunha finally got a **postal code** in 2005, but its approximately 270 residents see a mail ship only once a year.

FACT 591 Between 1880 and 1929, the Australian government kept caches of supplies on the remote **Antipodes Islands** for shipwreck survivors.

FACT 592 **There are more than two hundred dead bodies on Mount Everest.** The cold preserves the bodies from decay, and climbers use the more famous victims as landmarks.

FACT 593 👉 The island of Tuvalu in the South Pacific is so **small and remote** that the biggest building is a three-story administration building.

FACT 594 👉 In Supai, Arizona, located in the Grand Canyon, mail is still delivered by **mule train**.

FACT 595 👉 Scientists use the dry, dusty **Atacama Desert** in Chile to practice researching on Mars.

FACT 596 👉 The Kerguelen Islands in the southern Indian Ocean are a **six-day boat ride** from Madagascar, and their only inhabitants are French scientists.

FACT 597 👉 At a daunting 24,836 feet in elevation, Bhutan's Gangkhar Puensum—or "three mountain siblings"—is **the world's highest unclimbed mountain**.

FACT 598 👉 Cold and remote, the northern Siberian taiga **stretches over sixty-two thousand square miles**, a quarter of Russia's territory. There are no known inhabitants in these rarely explored woodlands, which are similar in density to Amazonian jungles.

FACT 599 👉 Siberia's northern forests are so remote that one family, the Lykovs, were **lost in it for forty-two years** until their chance discovery in 1978 by geologists.

FACT 600 👉 **The Amazon rain forests of Brazil are so vast that in 2011, the Brazilian government discovered a never-before-contacted tribe living deep in the jungle near Peru.**

FACT 601 👉 Ittoqqortoormiit, Greenland, is one of the most remote inhabited places in the Western Hemisphere. For nine months of the year the town is **only accessible by helicopter**.

FACT 602 👉 The Amundsen-Scott South Pole Station gets **six months of round-the-clock sunlight and six months of total darkness**.

FACT 603 👉 Once one of the most densely populated places on earth, Japan's Hashima Island has been **completely uninhabited** since undersea coal-mining operations were ceased there in 1974.

FACT 604 👉 Hashima Island was featured in a 2009 episode of the History Channel's show *Life After People* as an example of the **rapid decay of concrete buildings** only thirty-five years after abandonment.

FACT 605 👉 Access to Hashima is strictly limited today due to the **danger of crumbling ruins** on the island.

FACT 606 👉 During World War II, **mining work** on Hashima was done by forced Korean laborers and Chinese prisoners of war.

 are you sh*tting me?

18

Cryptids
Or Creatures You Don't Want to Believe Exist

BIGFOOT. THE LOCH NESS monster. Chupacabra. Mothman. They and their kind are called cryptids, which the field of study known as cryptozoology defines as creatures or plants whose existence has been suggested but not proven by the scientific community.

Some chalk them up to folklore and myth, while others want to believe. Me, I lean toward skepticism, although the more I read about these alleged creatures, the more I wonder if they might exist after all. The chupacabra has already been proven real—why not Bigfoot or Nessie?

If they are real, I'll tell you this: I don't want to bump into any of them on a dark night.

FACT 607 One argument that creatures can exist on earth without our knowledge comes from people such as cryptozoolist and author Loren Coleman, who points out that we have continued to discover new species since Baron Georges Cuvier, considered the father of paleontology, famously declared in 1812 that the world had **"little hope of discovering new species."** Since then, Coleman says, we have discovered the American tapir (1819), the giant squid (1870s), the okapi (1901), the Komodo dragon (1912), the kouprey (1937), and the ultimate "living fossil," the coelacanth (1938).

FACT 608 Supporters of the existence of cryptids also cite the case of Tibet's **giant panda**, which existed for more than seventy-five years between its discovery and first live capture.

FACT 609 East African natives spoke of a monster ape for decades before Belgian army captain Friedrich Robert von Beringe **killed two mountain gorillas** on Mount Sabyinyo in 1902, proving the legend true.

FACT 610 Native American folklore containing stories of a **Bigfoot-like creature** predates the arrival of the Europeans in North America.

FACT 611 *Sasquatch* comes from the Native American Salish word *se'sxac*, meaning **"wild men."**

FACT 612 Bigfoot-like creatures have been **sighted all over the world**, and under various names, including Sasquatch (United States), yeti (Himalayas), yowie (Australia), baramanu (Pakistan), yeren (China), and hibagon (Japan).

FACT 613 Fossil evidence shows that a Bigfoot-like creature called *Gigantopithecus* did exist **one to nine million years ago** and is most likely the ancestor of today's Sasquatches, if they exist.

FACT 614 👉 **The closest living relative of Gigantopithecus is the orangutan,** which shares some of the characteristics that eyewitnesses attribute to Sasquatch: long, reddish-brown hair, intelligence, and curiosity about human behavior.

FACT 615 👉 The modern legend of the **Loch Ness monster** was born when a sighting made local news on May 2, 1933, but accounts of an aquatic beast living in Scotland's Loch Ness date back twenty-five hundred years.

FACT 616 👉 Loch Ness monster scholars find numerous references to **"Nessie"** in Scottish history, dating back to around 500 C.E. when local Picts carved a strange aquatic creature into standing stones near Loch Ness.

FACT 617 👉 The **earliest written reference** to a monster in Loch Ness is a seventh-century biography of Irish missionary St. Columba.

FACT 618 👉 Enthusiasts believe that **a now-famous 1934 photograph** depicts a long-necked creature similar to a dinosaur rising from Loch Ness. Some take this as evidence that "Nessie" is the last living plesiosaur.

FACT 619 👉 **No conclusive scientific evidence exists** to prove the Nessie myth true, though many have tried using sonar and other tools.

FACT 620 👉 Stories of a **yeti**, or abominable snowman, have existed in the Himalayan regions of Tibet and Nepal since the fourth century B.C.E.

FACT 621 👉 The term **abominable snowman** first appeared in the press in 1921, when a journalist wrote about a sighting by explorer Charles Howard-Bury of large dark forms twenty thousand miles up in the Himalayas.

FACT 622 👉 Howard-Bury provided the first credible sighting of a yeti. His group later found footprints "**three times** those of normal humans" at the spot where the animals had been spotted.

FACT 623 👉 The yeti is known as **rakshasa**, or "demon," in ancient Sanskrit.

FACT 624 Believed to be not one creature but many, yetis are thought to be **intelligent enough to make tools and avoid humans**.

FACT 625 As interest in mountaineering has increased, so has the number of people who have **allegedly seen yeti tracks or the yeti itself**.

FACT 626 Typically reliable sources such as Sir Edmund Hillary and Tenzing Norgay even **claimed they saw giant footprints**, although Hillary later said he was skeptical about the source of the prints.

FACT 627 During a 2002 discussion on National Public Radio about crypto-primates like Sasquatch and the yeti, famed primatologist Dr. Jane Goodall said, **"I'm sure they exist."**

are you sh*tting me?

FACT 628  Despite long-standing myths of **dangerous, fanged creatures** that attack and drink the blood of livestock, scientists recently discovered that chupacabras are simply wild dogs and coyotes with a severe form of mange.

FACT 629 The legend of the **chupacabra**—Spanish for "goat sucker"—originates from Puerto Rico and Mexico, where there were a growing number of reports of attacks on livestock, specifically sheep, which were discovered dead, completely drained of blood.

FACT 630 The legend spread to other areas in Latin America and the United States, along with reports describing "**evil-looking animals** with long snouts, large fangs, scaly greenish-gray skin, and a nasty odor."

FACT 631 Experts say that animals inflicted with this form of mange would be quite debilitated and might resort to **attacking livestock** rather than their usual wild prey for an easier meal.

FACT 632 **The Mothman legend** centers around the collapse of the Silver Bridge in Point Pleasant, West Virginia, on December 15, 1967, which killed forty-six people. For thirteen months before the incident, dozens of people reported sightings of a huge, semihuman winged creature in and around Point Pleasant.

FACT 633 **Many claimed to have seen the creature**, dubbed "Mothman" by local media, not far from the bridge, leading to speculation that it was somehow involved with the bridge's collapse.

FACT 634 Most Mothman sightings described a **shadowy creature** standing six to seven feet tall with a ten-foot wingspan and large glowing red eyes.

FACT 635 👉 The creature reportedly **flies using bat-like wings to glide** rather than flap, and has the ability to fly great distances at speeds of up to a hundred miles per hour.

FACT 636 👉 The most well-known Mothman sighting occurred in November 1966 when **the creature reportedly appeared to two couples necking in a car** at an abandoned factory. The four witnesses saw a large animal shaped like a man, with glowing red eyes and big wings folded against its back.

FACT 637 👉 Other theories suggest that sightings of Mothman can be attributed to **a large bird like a sandhill crane**, which can grow to be over three feet tall with a wingspan of six feet.

FACT 638 👉 Shortly after the Silver Bridge collapsed, **Mothman seemed to quietly disappear**, and the sightings stopped.

FACT 639 👉 Some victims of the Silver Bridge collapse were Mothman witnesses, leading some to speculate that **the creature might have been trying to warn of the impending disaster**.

FACT 640 According to cryptozoologist and author Loren Coleman, the legend of the **Jersey Devil** dates back to at least 1735, when a woman in southern New Jersey is said to have given birth to a cursed child who grew to become the beast.

FACT 641 The Jersey Devil has been reported to be **as tall as eight feet** and is said to have a dog's face, a kangaroo's body, huge leathery wings, clawed hands, cloven hooves, and a forked tail.

FACT 642 Perhaps the creature's most frightening trait, however, is its fabled **"bloodcurdling scream."** Which would be my most frightening trait, too, if I saw this fucker in the woods.

FACT 643 **Explanations of the Jersey Devil range from suggestions that the creature is actually a remnant dinosaur species** or an undiscovered animal species to the belief that the monster is a mud-covered man living in the wild.

FACT 644 👉 The most credible Jersey Devil sighting occurred in 1993, when a park ranger on patrol in the Wharton State Forest came face-to-face with a large dark figure that stood over six feet tall and glared at him with **piercing red eyes**.

FACT 645 👉 **Sightings of the Jersey Devil continue to occur**, with one as recently as 2008 in Litchfield, Pennsylvania.

FACT 646 👉 "Champ" or "Champy" is the **resident aquatic monster** of Lake Champlain, between New York and Vermont.

FACT 647 👉 Champ sightings date back to the days when only Native American tribes lived in the area. Even the lake's namesake, Samuel de Champlain, noted in a 1609 journal entry that he had observed an unusual **twenty-foot-long serpentine creature** in the water.

FACT 648 Could Champ be a leftover dinosaur? Some eyewitness descriptions of the beast as a dark, long-necked, round-bodied creature up to thirty feet in length sound **eerily similar to a prehistoric plesiosaur**.

FACT 649 The *Skeptical Inquirer* says that an amateur photo of Champy taken by a woman named Sandra Mansi in 1977 "stands alone as **the most credible and important photographic evidence** for a lake monster in Champlain— or anywhere else."

FACT 650 Some Australians believe in semiaquatic creatures called **bunyips** that live in bodies of water in the outback.

FACT 651 The bunyip, which means **"bogey," "devil," or "spirit"** in an Aboriginal language, is described as being the size of a calf, dark brown in color, with the head of a horse and two large walrus-like tusks.

FACT 652 A legend of Australia's Aboriginal people, **bunyip have been sighted since the 1800s**. Such sightings were common in New South Wales, Victoria, and the Australian Capital Territory.

FACT 653 The legend of Kongomato describes a large flying beast, **similar to a bat or pterodactyl**, that roams sub-Saharan Africa attacking fishermen in small boats.

FACT 654 African locals describe the **flying beast** as having a long narrow head, a mouth full of sharp teeth, and a wingspan of up to seven feet.

FACT 655 One zoologist has theorized that the Kongomato is an exceptionally large species of the **hammerhead bat**, a particularly ugly fruit bat. Others have suggested that the flying creature is a surviving pterosaur.

FACT 656 Legend holds that a **giant anaconda** up to 50 meters (164 feet) long lives in the Amazon River. No proof has yet been produced that this creature, known as yacumama, or "mother of the water," exists.

FACT 657 Japan's version of the kraken is the akkorokamui, a **giant squid or octopus** that lurks in Funka Bay off the island of Hokkaido, reaching sizes of up to 110 meters. Funka Bay—wasn't that a Parliament album?

FACT 658 👉 Residents of East Anglia, UK, have feared a **terrifying black dog**, the Black Shuck, for centuries. Legend says that once you have gazed into the eyes of this demonic ghost dog, you will become ill or die soon afterward.

FACT 659 👉 The yowie, or doolagahl, which means "great hairy man," is **Australia's answer to Bigfoot**. Sightings dating back to the late 1880s describe an eight-foot-tall animal with a foul odor.

FACT 660 👉 **The yowie was most recently spotted in 1997 in Australia's Northern Territory. Police later found chewed water pipes and huge tracks where the creature had been seen.**

FACT 661 👉 Accounts of an unknown type of **giant earthworm** or snake called the minhocão began to circulate from Brazil in the eighteenth century. One writer in 1878 theorized that the animal could be a Pleistocene giant armadillo, the glyptodont.

FACT 662 🖝 At a reported two feet in circumference and up to five feet in length, the Gobi Desert's **Mongolian death worm** is not a creature you want to encounter without a change of underwear.

FACT 663 🖝 The death worm is said to **spit a toxic acid-like substance** and have the ability to shoot a deadly jolt of electricity from several feet away.

FACT 664 🖝 A **giant bat** called the ahool has been spotted in Java numerous times since 1924.

FACT 665 🖝 The ahool is said to resemble a **flying monkey** with long, sharp claws.

FACT 666 🖝 According to Caribbean legend, **the loogaroo are vampires** that were once old humans who made deals with the devil; they give him blood and he gives them magical powers in return.

FACT 667 👉 If a Caribbean islander awakens without any enthusiasm or energy, **he might suspect that a loogaroo has visited him during the night**, draining his blood and vital essence.

FACT 668 👉 The loogaroo are said to be **strangely compulsive**. You can thwart an attack by throwing grains of rice, seeds, peas, and other items on the ground, which the monsters will be compelled to stop and count. They are the Rain Men of the cryptid world.

19

Food Fails

"THIS CHAPTER IS THE worst!" my editor wrote in her notes on my original manuscript. *"Why are you telling me things?"*

Because I care, that's why, not just about my editor, but about you, dear reader. I don't want you to be surprised the next time you discover maggots in your mushrooms or antifreeze in your balsamic vinaigrette (or "vinegar-ette," as some people call it). I also figured you would want to know that the vanilla flavoring in some of your favorite foods comes from a beaver's butthole.

You're welcome.

FACT 669 For every dollar you spend on food, 19 cents goes to the actual food, while **the other 81 cents goes to marketing and packaging**.

FACT 670 According to University of Washington researchers, **two thousand calories' worth of fast/junk food costs $3.52 per day**; the same amount of nutritious foods costs closer to $36 per day.

FACT 671 The Institute of Brain Chemistry and Human Nutrition at London Metropolitan University discovered that, due to modern farm diets and living conditions, **chickens today contain 266 percent more fat than they did forty years ago**.

FACT 672 Because livestock is fed hormones, **cows produce double the amount of milk today than they did twenty years ago**. The hormone, recombinant bovine somatotropin (rBST), has been associated with many different types of cancer, including colon, prostate, and breast.

FACT 673 U.S. Food and Drug Administration (FDA) regulations on trans fats are incredibly lenient: a company can claim **zero trans fats** on a bag of snacks even if there is up to 0.49 gram per serving.

FACT 674 In the past forty years, **the number of allotted daily calories has increased by five hundred for the average American**. This translates to an extra fifty-two pounds per American per year.

food fails 189

FACT 675 👉 The U.S. Department of Agriculture (USDA) subcontracts a company to remove the potentially harmful bacteria in meat for products like fast-food hamburgers. The company **uses ammonia** to do the cleaning.

FACT 676 👉 The FDA allows for a can of mushrooms to include **more than twenty maggots** and seventy-five mites in every one hundred grams.

FACT 677 👉 Government data shows that every 500 grams of frozen berries—roughly the amount that goes into the average pie—can contain an average of four or more larvae and **ten or more whole insects**. Also, up to 60 percent of the berries can be moldy.

FACT 678 👉 **Four hundred or more insect fragments** and twenty-two or more rodent hairs are allowed in every hundred grams of ground cinnamon.

FACT 679 👉 Up to 10 percent of canned asparagus is allowed by the FDA to harbor **asparagus beetles or egg sacs**.

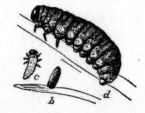

FACT 680 👉 The FDA says that **tomato paste** is inedible only if more than 45 percent of it is moldy.

- -

FACT 681 👉 As much as 5 percent of your maraschino cherries can **legally contain maggots**.

- -

FACT 682 👉 The FDA allows chocolate to contain up to **sixty insect parts** per hundred grams.

- -

FACT 683 👉 To create the turkey meat used in turkey burgers, patties, dogs, and nuggets, **an entire turkey**—including all of its bones and organs—is "mechanically separated from the bone." The mechanical separation process involves putting the turkey under high pressure to form a "paste-like and batter-like poultry product." *barf*

- -

FACT 684 👉 A food preservative called butylated hydroxytoluene (BHT) helps many of our foods from going bad, but it is **also widely used in embalming fluid and jet fuel**.

FACT 685  Sodium nitrite is used to stop the **growth of bacteria** in meat products. It is also a component of textile dyes.

FACT 686 There are 195 recognized countries in the world. Only 76 of them **do not have a McDonald's**.

FACT 687 McDonald's worldwide daily customer traffic (sixty-two million) **surpasses the population of Great Britain**.

FACT 688 McDonald's has **the world's sixty-eighth largest economy**, larger than Ecuador's.

FACT 689 An estimated **one in eight Americans has worked at a McDonald's** in his or her lifetime. Only half of them will admit it, though.

are you sh*tting me?

FACT 690 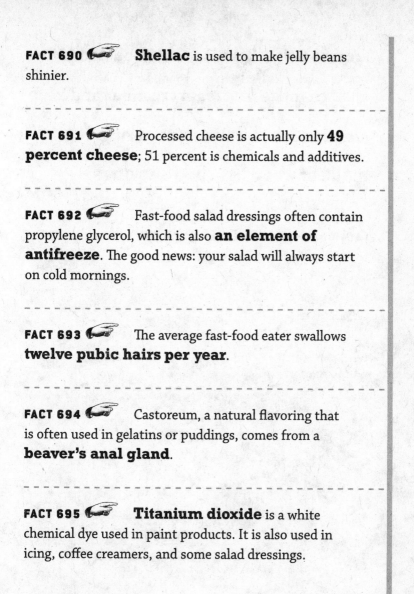 **Shellac** is used to make jelly beans shinier.

FACT 691 Processed cheese is actually only **49 percent cheese**; 51 percent is chemicals and additives.

FACT 692 Fast-food salad dressings often contain propylene glycerol, which is also **an element of antifreeze**. The good news: your salad will always start on cold mornings.

FACT 693 The average fast-food eater swallows **twelve pubic hairs per year**.

FACT 694 Castoreum, a natural flavoring that is often used in gelatins or puddings, comes from a **beaver's anal gland**.

FACT 695 **Titanium dioxide** is a white chemical dye used in paint products. It is also used in icing, coffee creamers, and some salad dressings.

FACT 696 ☞ Cellulose is a food additive used to make ice cream creamier and keep shredded cheese from separating. **It is made of wood pulp and shavings.**

FACT 697 ☞ **Animal bone char** is an ingredient used to make foods like sugar whiter.

20

Drivers Who Suck

WHEN WE TALK ABOUT crappy drivers, who are we really talking about? *Everyone but ourselves!* We are wonderful drivers, you and I. It's all these other idiots who go too fast or too slow or forget to use their turn signals or can't pick a lane, not us, right? Why can't they drive like you and I drive: perfectly?

When Albert Camus came up with the line, "Hell is other people," I bet he was driving. Hell is other people, all right: other people in their cars.

FACT 698 👉 Texting while driving has become **the leading cause of motor vehicle accidents and deaths for teenage drivers**. OMG! DOA!

FACT 699 👉 Driving a vehicle while texting is **six times more dangerous than driving while intoxicated**, according to the National Highway Traffic Safety Administration (NHTSA). Especially if you are texting something long like "the National Highway Traffic Safety Administration."

FACT 700 👉 NHTSA reports that sending or receiving a text takes a driver's eyes from the road for an average of 4.6 seconds. Moving at fifty-five miles per hour, this would be like **driving the length of an entire football field while blindfolded**.

FACT 701 👉 Texting in moving vehicles causes **more than 3,000 deaths and 330,000 injuries per year**, according to a Harvard Center for Risk Analysis study.

are you sh*tting me?

FACT 702  A texting driver is **twenty-three times more likely** to be involved in an accident than a driver who is not texting.

FACT 703 Speeding is a factor in **half of all fatal crashes** involving sixteen-year-old drivers with three or more passengers.

FACT 704 **Motor vehicle accidents are the number one cause of death** for Americans five to thirty-five years old. More than half of these accidents are caused by alcohol-impaired drivers.

FACT 705 In the United States, one life is lost **every twenty minutes** as a result of an alcohol-related car crash.

FACT 706 Alcohol-related accidents have resulted in the deaths of **more than 394,000 people in the past twenty years**.

FACT 707 👉 **More than 17,000 people are killed each year in alcohol-related accidents.** That's more than 325 a week and 46 every day.

FACT 708 👉 Our nation's capital is home to America's **most crash-prone drivers**. The average Washington, D.C., driver is involved in a crash once every 4.8 years, compared with a national average of once every ten years. If you've ever driven there, this won't surprise you.

FACT 709 👉 After Washington, D.C., **the most dangerous cities to drive in** are Baltimore, Maryland; Providence, Rhode Island; Hialeah, Florida; and Glendale, California.

FACT 710 👉 **According to a 2005 poll by the National Sleep Foundation, 60 percent of adult drivers—about 168 million people**—say they have driven a vehicle in the past year while feeling drowsy.

are you sh*tting me?

FACT 711 More than a third of those polled (37 percent or 103 million people) **admit to having fallen asleep at the wheel**. Of those who have nodded off, 13 percent say they have done so at least once a month.

FACT 712 Four percent—approximately eleven million drivers—admitted in the poll that they have had an accident or near accident because **they fell asleep or were too tired to drive**.

FACT 713 NHTSA estimates that driver fatigue is the cause of a hundred thousand police-reported crashes every year. **Accidents caused by drowsy driving** result in an estimated 1,550 deaths, seventy-one thousand injuries, and $12.5 billion in monetary losses per year.

FACT 714  In a recent study of turn signal usage by twelve thousand vehicles, the Society of Automotive Engineers (SAE) found that the **rate of turn signal neglect** for vehicles changing lanes is 48 percent. Vehicles making turns improperly used turn signals only 25 percent of the time.

FACT 715 The SAE extrapolated these findings to include all U.S. drivers, and the results suggest that turn signal neglect occurs more than **2 billion times a day**, or 750 billion times a year.

FACT 716 The study suggests that turn signal neglect is responsible for up to **2 million accidents per year**, more than twice the number of collisions caused by distracted driving.

FACT 717 The **deadliest bus accident** in American history happened in May 1988 when a church bus full of kids was hit head-on by a drunk driver going the wrong direction down Interstate 71 near Carrollton, Kentucky. Of the sixty-six passengers on the bus, twenty-seven died and thirty-four were injured, most of them severely.

are you sh*tting me?

FACT 718 The **drunk driver** who caused the Carrollton crash, Larry Wayne Mahoney, was sentenced to sixteen years in jail.

FACT 719 In 1990, **dense morning fog** was to blame for a seventy-five-car pileup on Interstate 75 in Tennessee that stretched for half a mile and caused fifteen deaths.

FACT 720 Signs warning motorists of fog had been posted in the area but were unreadable after foggy conditions **deteriorated too rapidly**.

FACT 721 Seven people were killed on July 4, 1998, on Virginia's Interstate 81 when **a car hydroplaned** during a storm, sailed across the median, and collided head-on with a tractor trailer. The six people in the car and the truck driver died.

FACT 722 Ice and snow caused at least twenty automobile accidents in Washington County, Maryland, on January 19, 2009. The worst of these was a pileup involving **seven tractor trailers and thirty-five cars** that claimed two lives and injured thirty-five people.

FACT 723 👉 The worst auto accident in Virginia history happened on February 22, 2000, when a sudden snowstorm on Interstate 95 in Stafford County caused a **117-vehicle pileup** that killed one and injured thirty-one.

FACT 724 👉 While just under 4,900 female drivers died in **U.S. traffic accidents** in 2009, more than 11,900 American males died in automobile accidents in the same year.

FACT 725 👉 A recent study based on data from 1999 to 2004 shows that fatality rates for drivers **rise after age sixty-five**. The higher the pants, the higher the death toll.

FACT 726 👉 The fatality rate for drivers **age eighty-five and older** is almost four times higher than that of teen drivers.

FACT 727 👉 The U.S. Census Bureau estimates that there will be **9.6 million people** age eighty-five and older by 2030, 73 percent more than today.

are you sh*tting me?

FACT 728 🖙 Elderly drivers are less likely to be in accidents caused by high speeds or alcohol, but more likely than other drivers to get into collisions when **missing a stop sign or turning into oncoming traffic**.

FACT 729 🖙 George Russell Weller, then eighty-six, killed ten people and injured more than seventy when he drove his Buick Le Sabre into a crowded farmers' market in Santa Monica, California, in 2003. His attorneys explained that Weller had **confused his car's accelerator for the brake**. He was convicted of vehicular manslaughter with gross negligence.

FACT 730 🖙 A judge ruled that Weller was **too ill to be imprisoned** and sentenced him to probation and $101,700 in penalties. The case fueled a nationwide debate over how elderly drivers should be screened. Being able to tell the difference between the gas pedal and the brake would be a good place to start.

FACT 731 🖙 NHTSA defines aggressive driving as "the operation of a motor vehicle in a manner that endangers or is likely to endanger persons or property." **Aggressive driving is a traffic offense**, not a criminal one.

FACT 732 Examples of **aggressive driving** cited by NHTSA include speeding or driving too fast for conditions, improper lane changing, tailgating, improper passing, or having those obnoxious plastic testicles hanging off the back of your truck.

FACT 733 Road rage can have fatal consequences. When a forty-nine-year-old Houston man blew his horn at a car that cut him off in 2010, the other driver chased the man down the freeway and **shot him to death**.

FACT 734 Two men were injured, one critically, when an October 2013 fender bender involving a motorcycle and a Range Rover on the Henry Hudson Parkway in New York City **erupted into road rage**. The Range Rover was chased by at least thirty bikers and cornered in traffic; the driver was pulled from his vehicle by several bikers and beaten in front of his family.

FACT 735 Road rage and aggressive driving cause **eight hundred deaths a year** on British roads, according to a 2010 survey by insurance company AXA.

are you sh*tting me?

FACT 736 More than half of the AXA survey respondents had been subjected to a "significant" act of road rage—shouting and aggression, not just a honk of the horn or a hand gesture.

FACT 737 Fifty-three percent of survey respondents admitted to behaving aggressively behind the wheel "sometimes," while nearly 20 percent admitted to **behaving aggressively "often."**

FACT 738 In 2013, the state of Ohio was ordered to pay more than $3 million for **failing to fix potholes** after the 2008 death of a Columbiana County nurse. The forty-nine-year-old woman was killed when a truck hit potholes and swerved head-on into her vehicle.

FACT 739 In November 1991, seventeen people were killed and 150 were injured when **blinding dust storms** across Interstate 5 near Coalinga, California, sent ninety-three cars and eleven tractor trailers smashing into one another in one of the worst chain-reaction accidents in U.S. history.

FACT 740 👉 From 1996 through 2000, 1,753 people died and thousands more were injured in **wrong-way crashes** on America's freeways.

FACT 741 👉 Wrong-way crashes generally result in a **high proportion of deaths and serious injuries**.

FACT 742 👉 In June 2002, a van carrying twenty-seven suspected illegal immigrants drove into oncoming traffic **with its headlights off** on Interstate 8 east of San Diego. The van crashed head-on into an SUV, killing six people and seriously injuring several others.

21

The 1970s, Man

IF YOU DON'T THINK the 1970s were scary, you weren't there. I was, and I remember when my parents stopped letting my sister and me watch the nightly news because it became too frightening for children. It was too frightening for everyone, really, these endless stories about the Vietnam War, demonstrations, shootings at Kent State, Watergate, the "Saturday Night Massacre," Munich, the PLO, the Manson family, Patty Hearst and the SLA, the Iran hostage crisis, the oil crisis, and more. No wonder everyone was doing drugs back then.

FACT 743 Stephen King came up with the idea for *Carrie* while cleaning the women's locker room in **his job as a school janitor**. He probably came up with *Misery* while cleaning the men's.

FACT 744 In 1974, local news reporter Christine Chubbuck shot herself on live television in Sarasota, Florida, making her **the first suicide broadcast on TV**.

FACT 745 Chubbuck had **a script that described the shooting** in the third person, accurately predicting how she was taken to the hospital in critical condition.

FACT 746 The Vietcong put

explosives in empty soda cans after

noticing that American soldiers liked to

kick them as they walked.

FACT 747 👈 Of the four students shot and killed by National Guardsmen at Kent State University in 1970, **only two were participating in antiwar demonstrations** at the time. The other two students were walking to class.

FACT 748 👈 At 4:00 A.M. on May 9, 1970, President Richard Nixon made an unplanned visit to the Lincoln Memorial to chat with antiwar protestors gathered there. The head of his Secret Service detail described it in his diary as **"the weirdest day so far."** Which, in the Nixon White House, was saying something.

FACT 749 👈 Before the shootings at Kent State, President Nixon was quoted **complaining about student protesters**, calling them "bums . . . blowing up campuses."

FACT 750 Some people suggested that actor Ben Stein was the **Watergate whistleblower "Deep Throat."** Stein was a speechwriter for President Nixon at the time. He can be seen crying in footage of Nixon's resignation speech to his staffers.

FACT 751 All American currency was **backed by gold** until 1971, when President Nixon passed a series of laws that canceled the direct convertibility of the United States dollar to gold and ushered in the era of freely floating currencies that remains to the present day.

FACT 752 Thirty-seven hundred people were arrested during the 1977 blackout in New York, the **biggest mass arrest in the city's history**.

FACT 753 During the **1977 New York City blackout**, looters and vandals caused $300 million worth of damage, breaking into more than sixteen hundred businesses and setting more than a thousand fires.

FACT 754 In the days leading up to the **1972 Munich Olympics**, security expert Dr. Georg Sieber warned Munich officials of the possibility of a terrorist attack eerily similar to the one that would occur at the games. His advice was ignored.

FACT 755 **Security was purposely lax** at the Munich Olympics. German officials hoped to present a more unthreatening and carefree image of their country than the world had last seen at the 1936 games there during Hitler's reign.

FACT 756 At the Munich Olympics, American athletes **unknowingly helped Palestinian terrorists gain access** to the Olympic Village.

FACT 757 In 1979, an unlikely series of mechanical and human errors at the **Three Mile Island nuclear plant** near Harrisburg, Pennsylvania, caused a partial meltdown of the reactor core and a release of significant amounts of radioactive gases into the atmosphere.

FACT 758 👉 The **near-total devastation** of the nuclear power industry resulted, as the disaster at Three Mile Island tipped the scales in the ongoing controversy over nuclear power in favor of those opposed to it.

FACT 759 👉 Massive demonstrations followed the Three Mile Island accident, culminating in a rally in New York City that attracted upward of **two hundred thousand people**. By the mid-1980s, the construction of nuclear power plants in the United States had virtually ceased.

FACT 760 👉 On November 4, 1979, a group of **Iranian students stormed the U.S. Embassy** in Tehran, taking more than sixty American hostages.

FACT 761 👉 The immediate cause of the Iran hostage crisis was President Jimmy Carter's decision to **allow Iran's deposed Shah into the United States** for medical treatment, but the event was also a dramatic way for student revolutionaries to break with Iran's past and put an end to American interference in its affairs.

 are you sh*tting me?

FACT 762 👉 **Iranian students freed their American hostages** on January 21, 1981, 444 days after the crisis began and just hours after newly elected president Ronald Reagan was sworn into office.

FACT 763 👉 In one of the most horrific incidents of violence against civilians during the Vietnam War, **a company of American soldiers killed the majority of the population of the South Vietnamese hamlet of My Lai** in March 1968.

FACT 764 👉 Though exact numbers remain unconfirmed, it is believed that as many as five hundred people, including women, children, and the elderly, were killed in the **My Lai massacre**.

FACT 765 👈 In 1970, a U.S. Army board charged fourteen officers with crimes related to the events at My Lai; **only one was convicted**.

FACT 766 👈 The brutality of the My Lai killings and the extent of the cover-up exacerbated **growing antiwar sentiment** in the United States and further divided the nation over the continuing American presence in Vietnam.

FACT 767 👈 On February 4, 1974, Patricia Hearst, the nineteen-year-old granddaughter of publishing billionaire William Randolph Hearst, was kidnapped from her Berkeley, California, apartment by the **Symbionese Liberation Army** (SLA), a radical activist group.

FACT 768 👈 Two months after her abduction, a gun-toting **Patty Hearst** was seen on security cameras participating in the SLA's armed robbery of a San Francisco bank. A taped message from the SLA soon followed in which Hearst claimed she had voluntarily joined the group and changed her name to "Tania."

FACT 769 👉 After police and FBI **killed most of the SLA members** in a shootout in Los Angeles in May 1974, Hearst disappeared for over a year before she was found in September 1975.

FACT 770 👉 Despite her argument that she had been coerced into joining the SLA through **repeated rape, isolation, and brainwashing**, Patty Hearst was convicted of armed robbery in 1976.

FACT 771 👉 President Jimmy Carter commuted Patty Hearst's sentence after she had served **almost two years in prison**. She was later pardoned by President Bill Clinton in January 2001.

FACT 772 👉 In 1978, former board of supervisors member Dan White **shot and killed** Mayor George Moscone and Supervisor Harvey Milk at City Hall in San Francisco, California. White had reportedly been angry about Moscone's decision not to reappoint him to the city board.

FACT 773 👈 Harvey Milk was one of the nation's first **openly gay politicians** and a much-admired activist in San Francisco. His and Moscone's murders were followed by demonstrations—some of them violent—as the city publicly mourned their loss.

FACT 774 👈 Dan White pleaded a **"diminished capacity" defense**, claiming that distress over losing his job caused him to suffer mental problems. In 1979, White was found guilty of voluntary manslaughter rather than murder and sentenced to just seven years in jail.

FACT 775 👈 White's sentence caused such **widespread public outrage** that California revoked the diminished capacity defense in subsequent cases.

FACT 776 👈 Dan White was released from prison in 1984 after serving **five years of his sentence**. He was unable to resume a normal life, and committed suicide in 1985.

are you sh*tting me?

22

The 1980s— OMIGOD!

YOU KNOW WHAT WAS frightening about the 1980s? I mean besides Cyndi Lauper and acid-washed jeans and Flock of Seagulls hair? The constant fear of nuclear annihilation, that's what. The Cold War got scalding hot in the 1980s, and there was a real fear that the Soviet Union was going to wipe us all out at any time. That's why I liked to live for the moment, and why I kissed that girl I barely knew at a frat party one night in 1983. After which she threw up all over me. Talk about rejection. Worse, she got barf on my Member's Only jacket. That was my favorite jacket, and I had to cut off the epaulets because they stunk like vomit. I was not happy about that.

FACT 777 The crew of the doomed 1986 *Challenger* **space shuttle** launch likely did not die in the initial explosion, but survived the three-minute fall to the ocean that destroyed the cabin on impact.

FACT 778 The ill-fated *Challenger* shuttle launch was not shown live on the major broadcast networks, which meant that many of the viewers who saw the shuttle explode on television were **young students watching the launch at school** via live NASA feeds.

FACT 779 Caroll Spinney, the puppeteer who voices **Big Bird, Oscar the Grouch, and other muppets** on *Sesame Street*, was offered a spot on the *Challenger* space shuttle, but when NASA realized there was no room for the Big Bird puppet in the craft, Spinney's spot was given to teacher Christa McAuliffe.

are you sh*tting me?

FACT 780 At Michael Jackson's request, the music video for "Beat It" featured **actual rival gang members**.

FACT 781 A planned duet album with Freddie Mercury and Michael Jackson was canceled in part because **Jackson brought a llama to a recording session.** Jackson also reportedly objected to Mercury's copious cocaine use. This sounds like the beginning of a joke: "Michael Jackson, Freddie Mercury, and a llama walk into a recording session. . . ."

FACT 782 In 1989, the Broward County sheriff's office **manufactured its own crack** to use in sting operations.

FACT 783 After the 1981 **assassination attempt on President Ronald Reagan**, Secret Service agents did not realize that Reagan had been shot until after they were in the limo headed for the White House.

FACT 784 President Ronald Reagan **lost half of his blood** after being shot in the 1981 assassination attempt.

FACT 785 In 1980, sportscaster Howard Cosell announced **John Lennon's death** during a Sunday night football game between the Patriots and the Dolphins.

FACT 786 Because blood-clotting medicine was made with donated blood platelets through the early 1980s, **huge numbers of hemophiliacs**—between 70 and 90 percent—were infected with AIDS before the medication was changed in 1985.

FACT 787 In 1989, a German official inadvertently opened the borders between East and West Berlin: he announced a planned change too early, which Berliners understood to mean that they could travel freely. **Thousands of East Berliners rushed through the wall**, too many for guards to stop.

FACT 788 The **Vietnam Veterans Memorial** was created in 1982 without any government funding.

are you sh*tting me?

FACT 789 👉 **Names are still being added** to the Vietnam Veterans Memorial; these are veterans who died from war-related injuries or causes.

- -

FACT 790 👉 The initial explosion in the 1986 **Chernobyl nuclear disaster** blew the thousand-ton cover off the reactor.

- -

FACT 791 👉 When officials evacuated the town of Pripyat near the site of the Chernobyl disaster, they told citizens they could come back soon, so **most people left their belongings and valuables behind**.

- -

FACT 792 👉 Within four months of the accident, **twenty-eight Chernobyl workers died**, some of whom heroically exposed themselves to radiation to protect the plant from additional leaks.

FACT 793 👉 Despite the contamination of the site—and the inherent risks in operating a reactor with serious design flaws—**the Chernobyl nuclear plant continued to operate for years after the disaster**. The last reactor was finally shut down in December 2000.

FACT 794 👉 The nuclear plant, the ghost towns of Pripyat and Chernobyl, and a large area surrounding the plant known as the **"zone of alienation"** are largely off-limits to humans. Because of the radiation in the region, the area won't be safe for human habitation for at least twenty thousand years. Mark your calendars.

FACT 795 👉 **When Mount Saint Helens in Washington erupted in 1980, volcano scientist David A. Johnson radioed the excited message, "This is it!" from his post beneath the volcano. It was his last message before he was killed by the eruption**. That was it, all right.

 are you sh*tting me?

FACT 796 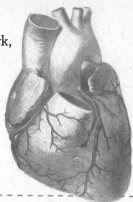 Though Barney Clark, the **first man to receive an artificial heart** in 1982, lived for 112 days after the surgery, his final months were uncomfortable, filled with media frenzy and painful infections.

FACT 797 In 1987, Bill Gates became the **youngest billionaire ever** at age thirty-one.

FACT 798 In 1981, daredevil Dan Goodwin **dressed up as Spider-Man** and climbed all the way up Chicago's Sears Tower.

23

Erectile Dysfunction Medication

IF THIS CHAPTER CAUSES you to have a flaccid penis for more than 168 hours, consult your doctor and tell him you've been reading books about scary facts.

FACT 799 🖙 **Viagra may be the next new thing in cancer treatment.** The combination of sildenafil citrate (the drug in Viagra) and the cancer drug doxorubicin has been shown to shrink cancerous tumors.

FACT 800 🖙 **The CIA trades ED drugs** to aging Afghan warlords and chieftains in exchange for information.

FACT 801 🖙 According to its manufacturer, Pfizer, **Viagra is the world's most counterfeited drug**.

FACT 802 🖙 **About 77 percent of Viagra purchased online is fake.** These are the ones we should be trading to the Afghan warlords.

FACT 803 🖙 In one month alone in 2013, customs officials at the airport in Miami, Florida, **confiscated 180,000 counterfeit Viagra pills**.

FACT 804 👉 Makers of counterfeit Viagra pills get the **signature blue color** by adding printer ink. Every pill is good for about thirty copies.

FACT 805 👉 Counterfeit ED drugs are seen as **"gateway drugs"** for smugglers. As a low-risk, high-yield product, smugglers escalate from erectile medications to counterfeit cancer drugs and antibiotics, which could lead to life-and-death consequences.

FACT 806 👉 Some erectile dysfunction medications can cause **hearing loss, cyanopsia (blue vision), and, in rare cases, permanent blindness**.

FACT 807 👉 For drug dealers, counterfeit sildenafil citrate can be better business than **selling hard drugs**, with profits up to two thousand times more.

FACT 808 👉 Sildenafil citrate is rumored to be the next **performance enhancer** for American football players. One player was quoted as saying he had heard of colleagues taking the drug to improve their game.

FACT 809   In September 2013, a Colombian man had to have invasive surgery on his penis after he took more than the recommended dose of Viagra. By the time he checked into the hospital, he had had an erection lasting several days, and **his penis suffered from inflammation, a fracture, and gangrene**.

FACT 810 A twenty-eight-year-old **Russian man died of a heart attack** in 2009 after taking a bet that he couldn't sexually satisfy two women for twelve hours. He overdosed on ED medication, won the bet, and died shortly after.

FACT 811 A man who injected himself with an excessive amount of erectile dysfunction drugs was so embarrassed by his **unyielding erection** that he delayed seeking medical attention. The overdose and delayed treatment left him with a penis that was under an inch long.

FACT 812 👉   A **priapism** is an erection lasting for more than four hours without sexual stimulation. It is named after the Greek god Priapus, whose penis was permanently erect.

- -

FACT 813 👉   One method of alleviating a priapism is to **insert a surgical shunt into the penis** to redirect the flow of blood. Another method is to read the previous sentence out loud.

- -

FACT 814 👉 **Another priapism treatment is aspiration of the penis**, or inserting a needle to drain blood from the organ.

- -

FACT 815 👉   In 2012, a fifty-two-year-old motorcyclist in California sued BMW—the maker of his bike—and the manufacturer of his motorcycle seat after suffering from a **two-year priapism** that he said began after a long ride in 2010. "He had to reconfigure his clothing," the man's attorney told the press, "and going to the bathroom was a problem." He had to install a toilet on the ceiling.

FACT 816 According to the *Journal of Sexual Medicine*, one treatment for erectile dysfunction may be found in the world's most deadly spider. The venom of the Brazilian wandering spider **contains a toxin that has been shown to improve erectile function.**

Drinks That Aren't Good for You

FACT: RESEARCHING THIS CHAPTER made me kick an eight-can-a-day soft drink addiction. It also reminded me of one of life's universal truths: there are no such things as shortcuts. I got hooked on soft drinks but didn't want to get fat, so instead of cutting back, I started drinking diet sodas instead. Guess what? Diet sodas make you even fatter. FAIL.

Go ahead and laugh at me if you like, then take a sip of that green tea you're drinking for antioxidants because you think it will replace all those vegetables you don't eat. Now I'm laughing at *you*.

FACT 817 According to the *American Journal of Clinical Nutrition*, children today drink diet soda "at **more than double the rate of the last decade**."

FACT 818 The consumption rate among adults is growing, too—we're **drinking almost 25 percent more diet sodas** than we did ten years ago.

FACT 819 Research is revealing that **diet drinks are not guilt-free at all**, but can stimulate your appetite and lead to weight gain, carbohydrate cravings, and excessive fat storage.

FACT 820 Consumption of diet soda is a large factor in the **mounting obesity crisis** that many countries now face.

are you sh*tting me?

FACT 821 👉 A study by the University of Texas Health Science Center showed that the **risk of becoming overweight** increases with the more diet sodas a person drinks.

FACT 822 👉 The University of Texas study followed 474 diet soda drinkers for nearly ten years and found that **their waists grew 70 percent more** than the waists of non–diet soda drinkers.

FACT 823 👉 In the same study, subjects who drank **two or more diet soft drinks a day** had a 500 percent greater increase in waist size over ten years than subjects who drank no diet soda.

FACT 824 👉 Our bodies aren't fooled by artificial sweeteners because they don't deliver anything to squelch the appetite, says one obesity researcher. Artificial sweeteners cause your body to **crave more sugar** "because your brain is not satisfied at a cellular level by the sugar impostor."

FACT 825 👉 According to a 2008 University of Minnesota study of almost ten thousand adults, even **just one diet soda a day** is linked to a 36 percent higher risk of metabolic syndrome, a group of symptoms that includes belly fat and high cholesterol, which puts you at risk for heart disease.

FACT 826 The sweetening agent in **Splenda**, sucralose, is made by adding three chlorine molecules to sugar molecules.

FACT 827 Studies have revealed that sucralose can **shrink the thymus glands** and enlarge your liver and kidneys. The sweetener has also been linked to atrophy of lymph follicles in the spleen and thymus, decreased red blood cell count, and diarrhea.

FACT 828 Some studies have suggested that **consuming aspartame can lead to headaches**.

FACT 829 Aspartame can **trigger or worsen numerous diseases**, including multiple sclerosis, epilepsy, Parkinson's disease, Alzheimer's disease, chronic fatigue syndrome, lymphoma, birth defects, fibromyalgia, and diabetes.

FACT 830 A Harvard Medical School study of more than three thousand women associated diet cola consumption with an **increased risk for kidney decline**. Kidney function started to diminish when women drank more than two sodas a day.

FACT 831 👉 Unlike regular soft drinks, **diet soda contains mold inhibitors**. These chemicals, which go by the names sodium benzoate or potassium benzoate, can cause severe damage to DNA in the mitochondria.

FACT 832 👉 According to the Center for Science in the Public Interest, mold inhibitors have also been connected to **allergic conditions such as hives and asthma**. Given a choice, I'll take hives over "severe damage to DNA in the mitochondria."

FACT 833 👉 Though some companies have replaced sodium benzoate with potassium benzoate, both preservatives were classified by the Food Commission in the United Kingdom as **irritants to the skin, eyes, and mucous membranes**.

FACT 834 👉 One study found similar levels of tooth erosion in the mouths of a person who used cocaine, a person who used crystal methamphetamine, and a person who habitually drank diet soda. **All three substances contain citric acid**, which can eat away at tooth enamel.

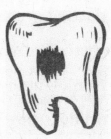

FACT 835 👉 According to a University of Michigan study, adults who drank three or more diet sodas a day had **worse dental health** than those who didn't. The diet soda drinkers experienced more problems, including more fillings, greater decay, and even missing teeth.

FACT 836 👉 Both diet and regular soft drink cans are lined with the endocrine disruptor bisphenol A (BPA), which has been **linked to heart disease, obesity, and reproductive problems**.

FACT 837 👉 Green tea consumers might not be getting the health benefits they expect from the drink. Some **bottled green teas** are packed with high fructose corn syrup, dyes, preservatives such as sodium benzoate and potassium sorbate, and numerous other chemical additives.

FACT 838 👉 **When you're drinking bottled green tea, you might not be getting as many antioxidants as you think—many commercial green tea products are little more than sugar water.**

FACT 839 While green tea has been **linked to weight loss and cancer prevention**, researchers have not been able to rule out other healthy behaviors as contributing factors.

FACT 840 In a study of green tea sold in stores, one variety was found to contain **almost no antioxidants**. Another bottled brand had only 60 percent of the amount of antioxidants listed on the label.

FACT 841 Leaves in two brands of green tea bags tested contained **1.25 to 2.5 micrograms of lead per serving**.

FACT 842 The green tea plant is **known to absorb lead** at a higher rate than other plants, and lead also can build up on the surface of the leaves.

FACT 843 **Industrial pollution in China**, where much green tea originates, is responsible for the presence of lead in those leaves.

FACT 844 👉 In 2012, the **energy drink industry** had estimated sales of more than $10 billion.

FACT 845 👉 Many energy drinks **do not label caffeine content** and can contain as much of the drug as fourteen cans of soda.

FACT 846 👉 The FDA limits caffeine content in soft drinks but imposes **no such rule** on energy drinks.

FACT 847 👉 Energy drinks can **increase blood pressure and stimulate the heart**, at times to the point of creating heart palpitations.

FACT 848 👉 Not only can caffeine raise your blood pressure and disrupt your sleep, but it can also **aggravate psychiatric conditions**.

FACT 849 👉 Excessive consumption can cause **caffeine intoxication**, which can lead to rapid or irregular heartbeat, difficulty breathing, convulsions, and vomiting.

FACT 850   A rising number of patients, many of them young people, are being treated in emergency rooms for complications related to **highly caffeinated energy drinks**, new federal data shows.

FACT 851   Complications from drinking energy drinks can include **anxiety, irregular heartbeats, and even heart attacks**.

FACT 852   **The number of annual hospital visits involving energy drinks doubled** from 2007 to 2011, according to a report by the Substance Abuse and Mental Health Services Administration.

FACT 853   In one study of people treated in the ER for complications related to energy drinks, more than 40 percent of them had consumed the beverages **with other alcohol and stimulants**, including Adderall and Ritalin.

FACT 854   The FDA **doesn't review energy drinks** because they are sold as dietary supplements.

FACT 855 **People who exercise shouldn't drink energy drinks.** The loss of fluid from sweating and caffeine can lead to dehydration.

FACT 856 **Energy drinks are popular with teens and young adults.** In a 2007 survey of 496 college students, 51 percent said they had consumed at least one energy drink during the past month.

FACT 857 **Energy drinks and alcohol are a dangerous match.** Since energy drinks are stimulants and alcohol is a depressant, mixing the two can give the illusion that you're not impaired.

FACT 858 Energy drinks do not lower your blood alcohol concentration (BAC) when mixed with alcoholic beverages. In fact, research has found the opposite: **people who combine alcohol and caffeine drink more and have higher BACs**.

FACT 859 After the stimulant effects of the energy drink taper off, the depressant effects of the alcohol are still in place, and can lead to **vomiting and respiratory issues**.

are you sh*tting me?

FACT 860 ☞ The **combined dehydrating effect of energy drinks and alcohol** can hinder your body's ability to metabolize alcohol and will increase the toxicity—and worsen your hangover—the next day.

FACT 861 ☞ In one study, college students who used energy drinks were more likely to use stimulants for recreational use, leading one Johns Hopkins University scientist to be concerned that **energy drinks are gateways to other types of drugs**.

FACT 862 ☞ Although energy drink manufacturers claim, or at least imply, that their drinks can have a positive effect on cognitive performance, studies have shown that consuming energy drinks has **no significant positive effect** on concentration, reasoning, or aptitude.

FACT 863 ☞ The results of two different university studies showed **no improved athletic performance** in participants who drank sugar-free energy drinks before testing.

FACT 864 ☞ Another study concluded that more than 44 percent of service members deployed in Afghanistan drank at least one energy drink per day. Nearly 14 percent drank **more than three energy beverages per day**.

FACT 865 ☞ Service members who drank three or more energy drinks per day tended to **sleep fewer than four hours per night** and were generally more stressed and tired.

25

Freak Accidents

LIFE IS SHORT, THEY say, and it's true. Life is also cruel, precarious, and wickedly ironic. One moment you're here, minding your own business, and the next you're as dead as Julius Caesar because some jerk decides to skydive off a building, his parachute fails, and he lands right on top of you and kills you. You don't even get a few seconds to say some final words, which in this case would be something like "*Are you fucking kidding me?!*"

FACT 866 👉 In 2007, a man walking down the street in Oakland, California, was killed when he was **struck in the head by a fire hydrant** that had been uprooted by a car crashing into it and propelled by water pressure.

FACT 867 👉 In 2010, Jimi Heselden, the multimillionaire owner of the company that makes Segway personal transporters, died after transporting himself over a cliff **on his Segway** and plunging eighty feet.

FACT 868 👉 A six-year-old boy died in July 2013 while undergoing a routine MRI exam at a New York–area hospital. The magnetic pull of the MRI machine caused a metal oxygen tank to fly across the room and **strike the child's head**.

FACT 869 👉 A spectator at a 1979 New York Jets football game died during a halftime model airplane exhibition when the pilot of a **miniature flying mower** lost control of his vehicle, which crashed into the audience.

FACT 870 👉 In 1995, **a female moose trampled a seventy-one-year-old man to death** on the campus of the University of Alaska in Anchorage. Witnesses said students had been throwing snowballs and harassing the moose and her calf for hours before the attack.

FACT 871 👉 In August 2013 in Panguitch, Utah, **a strong wind catapulted a trampoline** more than 150 feet through the air, killing a nine-year-old girl who had been sitting on it.

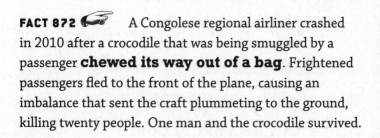

FACT 872 👉 A Congolese regional airliner crashed in 2010 after a crocodile that was being smuggled by a passenger **chewed its way out of a bag**. Frightened passengers fled to the front of the plane, causing an imbalance that sent the craft plummeting to the ground, killing twenty people. One man and the crocodile survived.

FACT 873 👈 Former Electric Light Orchestra member Mike Edwards was killed in 2010 when **a seven-hundred-pound hay bale rolled down an embankment** and onto the roof of his car, crushing him. Know who else hates those circular hay bales? Horses—they can't get a square meal anymore.

FACT 874 👈 Two people were killed and thirteen wounded in 2006 when an inflatable maze/bounce castle in Chester-le-Street, England, was **picked up by strong winds** and hurled across a public park.

FACT 875 👈 A stunt gone awry killed Canadian WWF wrestler Owen Hart during a televised event in 1999. A rig meant to lower Hart down to the ring from the rafters above malfunctioned, **dropping him seventy-eight feet to his death**.

FACT 876 👈 **An entire soccer team—eleven men—was killed instantly in 1998 when lightning struck their playing field during a match in the Democratic Republic of Congo.**

are you sh*tting me?

FACT 877 👉 In 2012, a Chicago waterfowl caretaker drowned **after being attacked by a swan** in a pond. Authorities believe that the man got too close to the bird or its nesting area.

FACT 878 👉 King Alexander of Greece died in 1920 when he received a **lethal infectious macaque bite** while defending his dog from an attack. Yep—a macaque attack put Al on his back.

FACT 879 👉 A youth athletics official in Düsseldorf, Germany, died **after being struck in the throat by a javelin** in August 2012.

FACT 880 👉 A four-year-old boy was killed in 2012 when **a six-foot-tall tombstone fell on him** in Utah's Glenwood Cemetery. The boy had been playing behind the statue when it fell.

FACT 881 👉 "To die, a momentous thing." Those were the final words sung by baritone Leonard Warren before he dropped dead on stage in 1960 from a **cerebral hemorrhage**.

FACT 882 👉 The final words sung by tenor Richard Versalle in 1996 were, "You can only live so long," after which he suffered a fatal heart attack and **fell off a twenty-foot-tall ladder.**

FACT 883 👉 Dancer Yoshiyuki Takada died on stage in 1985 when **the rope holding him upside down ripped apart**, dropping him six stories to his death. Strangely enough, his final performance was named "The Dance of Birth and Death."

FACT 884 👉 In March 2013, a popular coach at Rio Linda High School in Sacramento, California, died after running his bicycle into an open metal gate and **impaling himself.**

FACT 885 👉 A Manhattan advertising executive was **crushed to death** in 2011 after an elevator she was entering began to ascend with the doors open, trapping her against the shaft wall and dragging her up eight floors.

are you sh*tting me?

FACT 886 👉 An eerily similar accident occurred a year later, when New York City ad exec Suzanne Hart was crushed to death after **an open elevator began to move**.

FACT 887 👉 A nineteen-year-old model aircraft enthusiast in Queens, New York, was killed in September 2013 when **the miniature helicopter he was flying struck him in the head**.

FACT 888 👉 Spanish cyclist Xavier Tondo died in a bizarre accident in 2011. While trying to get his garage door open, Tondo's car rolled forward, **crushing him against the door**.

FACT 889 👉 Thirty-two members of the crew of the HMS *Trinidad* were killed in 1942 when **one of their own fired torpedoes circled around and struck them**.

FACT 890 👉 A Yale University chemistry student was killed in 2011 when her hair got caught in a laboratory lathe, a piece of machinery that spins very quickly, pulling her in. The cause of death was **accidental asphyxia by neck compression**.

FACT 891 👉 A twenty-five-year-old bride-to-be in Virginia Beach, Virginia, was paralyzed in 2010 when she was **pushed into the shallow end of a swimming pool** during a bachelorette party and hit her head on the bottom.

FACT 892 👉 The **four-year-old daughter of boxer Mike Tyson** was killed in 2009 after accidentally hanging herself with a treadmill cord in the family's Phoenix, Arizona, home.

FACT 893 👉 A Michigan woman was killed in 2008 after **a seventy-pound stingray leaped from the water** and impaled her through the neck with its barb. The woman had been sunbathing on a boat deck when the incident occurred.

FACT 894 👉 In a prank gone horribly wrong, a New York teenager died in September 2013 while trying to surprise a friend. The girl jumped out of a closet and was **shot by the friend**, who mistook her for an intruder.

are you sh*tting me?

FACT 895 👉 In 1814, **a 135,000-gallon beer vat ruptured** at Meux & Co.'s Horse Shoe Brewery in London, starting a chain reaction of overturned vats that caused eight drownings.

FACT 896 👉 In July 2013 at Panama City Beach, Florida, two vacationing teenagers were seriously injured in a **freak parasailing accident**. A cord tethering the parasail snapped, sending the two girls careening into the side of a high-rise condo balcony. Don't you hate it when people drop in unannounced when you're at the beach?

FACT 897 👉 In March 2013, a **flight status display board** at Birmingham-Shuttlesworth International Airport in Alabama crashed down, killing a ten-year-old boy and injuring several members of his family.

FACT 898 👉 A central Florida man died in March 2013 when **a sinkhole opened underneath his home** and swallowed him as he slept in his bedroom. The man's body was never recovered.

FACT 899   A three-year-old Harlem girl was killed in September 2013 when the sofa bed on which she and her sisters were playing suddenly **snapped shut, suffocating her**.

FACT 900   A commuter in Lexington, Kentucky, died in July 2013 when a highway mowing crew ran over a softball-size rock as he drove by. **The rock shot through the man's car window and hit him in the face**, killing him instantly.

FACT 901   In Orlando, Florida, in 2012, a fifty-five-year-old man was killed when **the side-view mirror of a passing truck struck him in the head** as he mowed his lawn.

FACT 902   A seventeen-year-old boy was **electrocuted to death** while working at a Baltimore-area Circuit City store in 1995. Managers said James Hill was vacuuming when they heard a scream.

FACT 903   On a California highway in May 2013, **a three-foot-long metal pipe flew through a car's windshield**, killing the driver.

FACT 904 👉 In 2012 in Sydney, Australia, a truck carrying twenty-two tons of timber toppled over while turning a corner and **dropped its load on several cars** waiting for a light to change, instantly killing one driver.

FACT 905 👉 In 1976, seven motorists were killed and an additional 170 were injured when a truck carrying anhydrous ammonia overturned in Houston, Texas, releasing a **toxic cloud of fumes**.

FACT 906 👉 Five men working on a nineteen-hundred-foot radio broadcast tower died in Houston, Texas, in 1982 when **a guy wire was severed**, causing the structure to collapse.

FACT 907 👉 In 2003, a doctor at Houston's St. Joseph Medical Center was decapitated when **an elevator's doors closed on his head** and the car bolted upward.

FACT 908 🖅   In 2013, a fourteen-year-old boy died while playing hide-and-seek on the Texas Tech campus. The victim **accidentally ran into a large statue of a bull** and impaled himself on one of the horns.

FACT 909 🖅   A sixteen-year-old Queens, New York, boy died in 2012 after he **stuck his head out of the emergency hatch** atop a double-decker party bus and struck a freeway overpass.

FACT 910 🖅   A homeless Fort Worth, Texas, man died in July 2013 after falling asleep in a Dumpster and being **crushed to death by the compactor** of a sanitation truck.

FACT 911 🖅   In 2011, a Toronto, Canada, pasta company worker was killed when he fell off a ladder and **tumbled into an industrial dough machine** while it was still running.

26

Things That Stink and Then Kill You

HERE'S A TIP: A nasty smell is nature's way of telling you that whatever is in your nose at that moment is bad news. Whether it's a dog fart or volatile organic compounds, the stink says you should seek oxygen elsewhere before you asphyxiate. So listen to the stink and obey. Or die with that "I smell poo" look on your face. Your choice.

The more you know . . . *rainbow*.

FACT 912 The combination of bleach and ammonia produces chloramine gas, which can cause **coughing, choking, lung damage, and death**.

FACT 913 The strong initial smell of chloramine gas may be blocked due to a phenomenon called **nasal fatigue**, which can make it hard for people to detect increasing danger.

FACT 914 A strong foul smell called mercaptan is added to propane and natural gas, which have **no readily detectable odor**, to help people identify potentially fatal leaks.

FACT 915 If you **smell burning rubber**, it's a possible indication that something electrical—from overheated motors to overloaded extension cords—could be close to starting a fire.

FACT 916 While sewer and septic systems are mostly just smelly, **accumulations of gas** can be a health threat and even cause explosions.

FACT 917 When water **smells like rotten eggs**, the cause is typically hydrogen sulfide gas, which can cause health problems when highly concentrated.

FACT 918 Unchecked moisture in a home can lead to smelly mildew, which is produced by molds and emits **volatile organic compounds** (VOCs) that can be dangerous to your health and damage your home.

FACT 919 **Most new carpets contain VOCs** and emit them as strong-smelling gases that can cause a variety of health issues, from headaches and nausea to allergic reactions and dizziness.

FACT 920 **Carpets can also contain known carcinogens** such as *p*-dichlorobenzene, which can cause hallucinations, nerve damage, and respiratory illness in humans.

FACT 921 👉 The **new carpet smell** is courtesy of the chemical 4-phenylcyclohexene (4-PCH), which can cause eye and breathing problems.

FACT 922 👉 The retardant polybrominated diphenyl ether (PBDE), found in new carpeting, has been shown to **affect the human thyroid and immune systems** and damage brain development functions.

FACT 923 👉 Toxic carpet fumes are especially **dangerous for infants** and people with asthma, migraines, allergies, or other immune-compromised illnesses.

FACT 924 👉 Solvents and VOCs in household paint can **evaporate as toxic fumes** as the paint dries.

FACT 925 👉 **Inhaling paint fumes can exacerbate asthma and sinusitis.** As your body takes the paint solvents into your lungs and bloodstream, you can also experience headaches and dizziness.

FACT 926 Exposure to large quantities of **paint fumes** has been linked in animal studies to birth defects, cancers, and damage to the central nervous system.

FACT 927 According to the World Health Organization, professional painters have an increased risk of getting **different types of cancer**, in particular, lung cancer.

FACT 928 **"Painter's dementia"** is a neurological condition brought on by long-term exposure to paint solvents. Another kind of painter's dementia is thinking you should paint the room yourself because you can do as good a job as a professional, right? So why not save a few bucks? It'll be a fun project.

FACT 929 According to researchers at Sheffield University and Manchester University, men exposed to paint chemicals are **more likely to experience fertility problems**.

FACT 930 You can thank a buildup of bacteria in the mouth, lungs, and gut for **your dog's bad breath**. That, and the fact that he licks his own ass for hours on end.

FACT 931 Persistent bad breath can indicate that your dog needs better dental care or that something is wrong in his gastrointestinal tract, liver, or kidneys.

FACT 932 Dental or gum disease can cause **halitosis in dogs**, and certain dogs—especially small ones—are particularly susceptible to tartar and plaque buildup. It's hard to floss without thumbs.

FACT 933 When inhaled in sufficient amounts, **pesticides can damage the nose, throat, and lung tissues**, or can be absorbed through the lungs into the bloodstream. The most serious risks come from vapors and small particles.

FACT 934 If mishandled, the potentially deadly nitrogen-based gas anhydrous ammonia can burn, as well as cause **irritation in the eyes, nose, and throat**.

are you sh*tting me?

FACT 935 Neighbors of **concentrated animal feeding operations** (CAFOs) frequently complain about odors, and tend to experience higher levels of tension, fatigue, confusion, and depression.

FACT 936 Studies of people who live next to CAFOs also report **respiratory ailments, headaches, and nausea**.

FACT 937 Diesel engine exhaust adds soot and gas to the atmosphere, and has been **linked to cancer and lung and heart diseases**.

FACT 938 Studies show that workers who are regularly exposed to diesel exhaust have an **increased risk of lung cancer**.

FACT 939 Railroad workers, heavy equipment operators, truck drivers, and other workers with ongoing exposure to diesel exhaust have **higher lung cancer death rates** than those who aren't exposed.

FACT 940 Among the **foul-smelling gases produced in landfills**, ammonia, sulfides, methane, and carbon dioxide are of most concern.

FACT 941 Ammonia and hydrogen sulfide are responsible for most of the odors at landfills. Short-term exposure to **elevated airborne levels** of either of these compounds can cause coughing; headache; breathing difficulties; and irritation of the eyes, nose, and throat.

FACT 942 **Body odor** is caused by bacteria that feeds on the milky sweat produced by our apocrine glands, which are found under the arms and around the genitals.

FACT 943 Body odor that **smells like rotting garbage** can indicate that a tampon has been left too long in a woman's vagina.

FACT 944 👉 A vaginal discharge with a pasty, yeasty smell like bread dough is a sign that you have a **yeast infection** caused by an overgrowth of the naturally occurring fungus *Candida*.

FACT 945 👉 The growth of *Candida,* which occurs naturally in the vagina, is **kept in check by other bacteria**. But when this balance is disrupted—often by antibiotic use, pregnancy, diabetes, or a compromised immune system—a yeast infection can result.

FACT 946 👉 **Fetid urine** can point to a urinary tract infection (UTI) in the kidneys, bladder, ureters, and/ or urethra. Other symptoms of a UTI include burning, urgency, leaking, pain, and cloudy or bloody urine.

FACT 947 👉 **Strong foot odor** is called bromhidrosis, or smell caused by sweat. The sweat doesn't smell on its own but creates a moist environment ideal for the growth of bacteria and fungi, which cause the odor.

FACT 948 👉 Trimethylaminuria, also called TMAU or **fish odor syndrome**, is a rare metabolic disorder that results in a constant fishy body odor.

FACT 949   **Very little treatment is available** for fish odor syndrome. Low doses of antibiotics can alleviate some of the odor, but the smell often increases when people with TMAU eat eggs, beans, broccoli, or seafood. Or when anybody eats eggs, beans, broccoli, or seafood.

FACT 950   Stress, imbalanced hormones, heat, and exercise can lead to changes in body odor due to excessive sweating. Called **hyperhidrosis**, the condition affects the hands, feet, and armpits and inflames the skin.

FACT 951   Unusual changes in body odor can indicate the presence of **acromegaly**, a serious medical condition. These changes are caused by excessive hormone production in the pituitary gland, often because of a tumor pressing on the gland.

FACT 952   **Acromegaly can lead to death** if left untreated. Other symptoms include enlarged hands and feet, joint pain, deepening voice, high blood pressure, and vision loss.

are you sh*tting me?

FACT 953 The family of insects known as stinkbugs repulse their prey by **releasing a foul-smelling liquid**.

FACT 954 A typical smell of dental practices is that of **the antiseptic eugenol**, or oil of cloves. In one study, the smell was rated as pleasant by nonfearful dental patients, but unpleasant by fearful ones. These results seem to confirm the role of odors as elicitors of emotional memories.

FACT 955 *Pseudomonas* is a type of bacteria commonly found in water and moist areas that can produce a **foul-smelling infection** in humans and animals.

FACT 956 **Tear gas**, an irritant to mucous membranes in the eyes, nose, mouth, and lungs, is the active ingredient in Mace.

FACT 957 **Paleo or low-carb diets can cause bad breath.** A reduced amount of carbs causes the body to metabolize fat in an effort to fuel itself. Ketones, a smelly by-product of this process, are eliminated from the body through breath and urine.

FACT 958 If you're on antidepressants and other prescription drugs, **you may sweat more**, allowing odor-causing bacteria to thrive.

FACT 959 Saliva helps flush the mouth, so **medications that cause dry mouth can also lead to bad breath**.

FACT 960 **The molecular structure of a drug may play a role in unpleasant body odor.** Chemical compounds that contain large quantities of nitrogen and sulfur can increase your body odor.

FACT 961 **The liver and the kidneys detoxify the body**, so when their functioning is impaired, compounds can build up and produce unpleasant body odor.

 are you sh*tting me?

27

Doomsday Scenarios

THERE'S NO NICE WAY to say it: we're screwed. One way or another, we'll all be obliterated someday, and that day is sooner than you think. You know that TV show called *1000 Ways to Die*? That's how I felt when I was researching this chapter. We are screwed ten times over and ten more times after that. If a supervolcano doesn't get us, an asteroid will. If the asteroid doesn't get us, a comet will. If a comet doesn't wipe us out, it will be a global pandemic or a gamma-ray burst or a black hole or a nuclear holocaust, or even our own sun.

The good news is that whatever happens will probably be quick. That, and we won't have to hear about Miley Cyrus anymore.

FACT 962 Experts say that an eruption of a supervolcano, such as the one that lies beneath Yellowstone National Park, could occur soon and would be **catastrophic to our planet**.

FACT 963 Over the past decade, **Yellowstone's volcanic crater has risen ten inches**. Scientists believe that molten rock is accumulating underneath.

FACT 964 In the past two million years, the Yellowstone volcano has **erupted three times**, each one a thousand times more powerful than the 1980 eruption of Mount Saint Helens in Washington.

are you sh*tting me?

FACT 965 A volcanic eruption near Yellowstone two million years ago was **twenty-four hundred times more powerful** than the Mount Saint Helens blast, emitting six hundred cubic tons of dust and ash into the atmosphere.

FACT 966 Since that ancient blast, **massive eruptions** have taken place at Yellowstone about every 600,000 years, with the last one occurring 640,000 years ago. In other words, get ready.

FACT 967 Such an eruption today would equal the force of **a thousand Hiroshima-strength atomic bombs** exploding every second.

FACT 968 Fallout from a supervolcano could also put enough sunlight-blocking dust in the air to cause a **deep plunge in temperatures** on the earth's surface.

DANGER

FACT 969 Giant volcanic eruptions have contributed to **mass extinctions**, including the one that helped to kill off the dinosaurs around sixty-five million years ago.

FACT 970 Scientists have also shown that a Siberian volcano may have precipitated the largest extinction on record about 250 million years ago, as it belched out enough sulfur, carbon dioxide, and ash to **alter the climate and collapse the food chain**.

FACT 971 **Asteroids are the extraterrestrial objects most likely to strike Earth.** An asteroid at least 106 miles wide that crashed into what is now Mexico's Yucatán Peninsula is believed to have been partly responsible for the dinosaurs' extinction.

FACT 972 NASA predicts that an asteroid larger than fifty-five yards wide will **strike the earth roughly every hundred years**, potentially leading to floods and destruction of cities and farms.

FACT 973 👉 An **asteroid collision with Earth** would also create firestorms, acid rain that would kill crops, and debris that would shield the planet from sunlight, according to NASA's Near-Earth Object Program.

FACT 974 👉 A three-hundred-yard-wide asteroid called **99942 Apophis will pass within the orbits of Earth satellites** in 2029 and could strike our planet.

FACT 975 👉 Comets, moving through space at almost a hundred thousand miles per hour can be propelled even faster by the gravitational pull from Earth. The resulting force from a comet collision with Earth could **wipe out the human race**.

FACT 976 👉 Since comets are essentially **dark, dirty snowballs**, finding them in the outer reaches of the solar system can be difficult.

FACT 977 👉 Among the most powerful explosions in the universe, **supernovas can match the power of a few octillion nuclear warheads**. If you're wondering how many an octillion is, it's roughly 800 shitloads.

FACT 978 👉 Though most supernovas occur too far away from Earth to do any real damage, a supernova's radiation could theoretically **destroy the ozone** in the atmosphere, increasing the amount of ultraviolet (UV) light that gets through to catastrophic levels.

FACT 979 👉 A supernova's radiation could also cause a UV flash, which would damage the ozone, increase skin cancer rates, and kill off mass amounts of bacteria, essentially creating **another Ice Age**.

FACT 980 👉 When large stars die and collapse, powerful beams of energy burst from both poles, **shooting gamma rays** and charged particles that for a few seconds outshine the rest of the stars in the universe combined.

FACT 981 👉 The most powerful explosions known in the universe are gamma-ray bursts. A fiery pinwheel in space named WR 104, about eight thousand light-years away from Earth, could fire a gamma-ray burst in our direction, **potentially causing mass extinctions**.

FACT 982 Scientists predict that in about a billion years, **the sun will shine 10 percent brighter**, turning our planet into an oven. The earth's temperature will increase to well over 200°F, boiling off our oceans and collapsing our climate.

FACT 983 Solar flares, which are jets of plasma shooting out of the sun, can wreak havoc on today's vast interconnected power grid and cause **massive outages, radio blackouts, satellite malfunctions, telecommunication-system meltdowns**, and more.

FACT 984 The massive gravitational pull of Jupiter, our largest planet, could throw another planet in our solar system far enough off course to create a cosmic chain reaction that would result in a **collision between Mercury and Earth** and destroy us.

FACT 985 There is growing evidence to suggest that **wandering black holes exist** in our own galaxy, The holes are difficult to spot and carry more than enough energy to destroy Earth.

FACT 986 👆 One downside of the **Large Hadron Collider** in Switzerland is the possibility of its creating mini black holes, which could essentially dice the planet into pieces. English astrophysicist Martin Rees said there is a one in fifty million chance that it will happen.

FACT 987 👆 With a quarter of Earth's mammals facing extinction and 90 percent of our large fish already gone, **our planet's shrinking biodiversity** could spell our doom. At current rates of extinction, half of our animal species will be gone within a hundred years.

FACT 988 👆 According to a warning issued at the 2010 Convention on Biological Diversity, so dependent are humans on the interconnected services of plants and animals that **unless this loss of biodiversity is halted, humans will likely join this list of extinctions**.

FACT 989 👆 Soon it could be possible to design **babies whose DNA has been rewritten** to give them greater mental and physical abilities. A breed of their own, they'd only be able to mate with others of their kind—like hipsters, but without the ironic hats.

FACT 990 👉 Icy structures called clathrates at the bottom of the world's oceans contain **mass quantities of naturally occurring gases**, including methane. The warmer the oceans become, the more the clathrates will swell and belch their methane stores to the water's surface. The release of these greenhouses gases into the atmosphere will trigger more global warming and the release of yet more of the clathrates' gasses.

FACT 991 👉 According to the U.S. Department of Agriculture, a third of what we eat comes from plants that are pollinated by bees. Since 2006, honeybees have been dying off by the millions and experts don't know why. Without honeybees to help propagate our crops, **there will be a critical shortage to global food supplies.**

FACT 992 👉 **The 1918 influenza pandemic** killed 50 to 80 million people. Today, an equivalent globally disruptive pandemic would have a death toll of 210 million.

FACT 993   In 2011, the scientific community was outraged that **researchers engineered a mutant version of the bird flu H5N1** that was transmissible in ferrets and transmitted via the air. The results sparked fears that engineered deadly diseases could be accidentally or intentionally released, leading to a global pandemic.

FACT 994   When carbon dioxide levels in the atmosphere rose significantly million of years ago, our oceans became acidic, setting off **a wave of extinction**. Today, carbon dioxide levels are again soaring—but this time, they're rising ten times faster than before.

FACT 995   Damage from ocean acidification could be most visible in coral reefs, which would not only result in a loss of habitat for an estimated 25 percent of marine life but also **expose many coastal cities to greater storm and wave damage**.

FACT 996   Moore's Law is the observation that computer chips get twice as powerful every two years, leading to the implication that computer intelligence will eventually be **greater than human intelligence**. What we don't know is what the artificial superintelligence of the future will choose to do with its gifts.

FACT 997 👉   With **artificial brains**, one expert says, we could "get something that's very intelligent but has motivations that are completely nonhuman. [The computer] might not care about anything that we care about, but since it's smarter, it's going to get what it wants."

- -

FACT 998 👉   **Earth's magnetic field** decreases to almost nothing every few hundred thousand years, then, about a century later, reappears with the north and south poles reversed. The last switch was more than 700,000 years ago, so we are overdue.

- -

FACT 999 👉   Without magnetic protection, more particle storms, cosmic rays from the sun, and energetic subatomic particles from deep space would strike Earth's atmosphere, **eroding the already beleaguered ozone layer** and disrupting everything from power grids to gas pipelines to communications satellites.

- -

FACT 1000 👉   According to a 2010 Ploughshares Fund report, **twenty-two thousand active nuclear warheads are scattered around the globe**, more than enough to destroy the world. And that number doesn't include smaller weapons that are more susceptible to theft.

FACT 1001    In 1983, a secret satellite-monitoring facility near Moscow received a warning that **five nuclear missiles were launched** from the United States. Fortunately, the facility's officer questioned the reliability of new equipment, choosing to wait before setting off the alarm. The officer's judgment was sound—the alarm was false—and he likely saved the world from a nuclear war.

FACT 1002   Since the end of the Cold War, nuclear worries have subsided. However, the possession of nuclear weapons by **terrorist groups and rogue states** remains a worldwide concern.

FACT 1003   *Physics Today* published a study in 2008 that suggests "**a regional war involving as few as a hundred bombs could cause a nuclear winter**, resulting in the lowest temperatures in a thousand years, while an exchange involving thousands of weapons would . . . 'likely eliminate the majority of the human population.'"

FACT 1004   Most scientists think it won't be one doomsday event that wipes us out, but rather a **snowball effect**: smaller events degrading life gradually until it eventually becomes unsustainable.

are you sh*tting me?

SOURCES

1. FLORIDA

1. www.huffingtonpost.com/2012/12/06/mother-daughter-porn-duo-jessica-monica-sexxxton_n_2238052.html.
2. www.huffingtonpost.com/2012/12/29/jennie-scott-florida-arrested-oral-sex_n_2381876.html?utm_hp_ref=weird-florida.
3. www.news4jax.com/news/Police-Alanis-Morissette-music-leads-to-domestic-violence/-/475880/17008390/-/bum7kk/-/index.html; http://www.thesmokinggun.com/file/alanis-morissette-attack?page=0.
4. www.sun-sentinel.com/news/palm-beach/fl-machete-attack-20130719,0,4335746.story.
5. www.firstcoastnews.com/news/strange/article/318962/82/Man-rides-600-lb-aluminum-chicken-to-jail.
6. www.cfnews13.com/content/news/cfnews13/news/article.html/content/news/articles/cfn/2013/6/26/cops_man_put_nude_ph.html.
7. coastal.er.usgs.gov/stjohns/ofr616/kingsley.html.
8. www.abcactionnews.com/dpp/news/state/major-law-enforcement-response-to-juvenile-correction-facility-near-avon-park.
9. www.huffingtonpost.com/2013/09/13/herpes-monkeys-florida_n_3922247.html?utm_hp_ref=weird-florida; http://nypost.com/2013/09/12/herpes-infected-monkeys-terrorize-florida.
10. www.huffingtonpost.com/2013/08/30/giant-african-land-snails-florida_n_3839787.html.
11. Ibid.
12. Ibid.
13. www.huffingtonpost.com/2013/09/13/herpes-monkeys-florida_n_3922247.html?utm_hp_ref=weird-florida.
14. http://pythonchallenge.net.
15. www.huffingtonpost.com/2013/09/10/rock-python-dog-miami_n_3901281.html.
16. Ibid.
17. www.abc-7.com/story/23985685/collier-student-suspended-after-twerking-incident#.UrRfB6XZX1r.
18. www.wesh.com/news/central-florida/deputies-man-terrorized-8yearold-over-potato-chips/-/11788162/22791834/-/bw0o1k/-/index.html.

19. www.sun-sentinel.com/news/palm-beach/fl-alligator-beer-20131217,0,2355871.story.
20. http://blogs.miaminewtimes.com/riptide/2013/03/florida_keys_woman_bites_sprin.php.
21. http://tbo.com/news/breaking-news/12-foot-gator-tied-to-tree-behind-apartment-complex-20131024.
22. www.washingtonpost.com/blogs/answer-sheet/wp/2013/09/12/school-named-after-kkk-leader-asked-to-change-its-name.
23. www.huffingtonpost.com/2013/01/25/witnesses-suspects-praye_n_2547808.html?utm_hp_ref=weird-florida.
24. Ibid.
25. www.myfoxtampabay.com/story/20591712/2013/01/15/man-arrested-for-giving-people-wedgies.
26. www.rawstory.com/rs/2013/09/18/florida-man-beats-daughter-for-40-minutes-to-the-tune-of-blurred-lines.
27. http://blogs.miaminewtimes.com/riptide/2013/01/florida_man_bites_off_girlfrie.php.
28. www.clickorlando.com/news/man-attacked-pregnant-sister-over-chicken-nuggets-orlando-police-say/-/1637132/23071818/-/5g9skgz/-/index.html.
29. www.wtsp.com/news/watercooler/article/344460/58/Florida-woman-renews-marriage-vows-with-ferris-wheel.
30. www.wpbf.com/news/south-florida/not-homeless-need-boob-fla-woman-asks-for-donations-alongside-busy-roadway/-/8788880/21404850/-/aink3x/-/index.html.
31. www.nbcmiami.com/news/local/Man-Sprinkled-Fiancees-Ashes-at-LensCrafters-Causing-Florida-Malls-Evacuation-Sarasota-Police-228075171.html.

2. ANCIENT MEDICAL PRACTICES

32. http://health.howstuffworks.com/medicine/modern-treatments/maggot-therapy.htm.
33. Ibid.
34. Francesca Gould, *Why You Shouldn't Eat Your Boogers and Other Useless Information about Your Body* (Tarcher/Penguin, 2007).
35. Ibid.
36. Ibid.
37. Ibid.
38. Ibid
39. www.history.com/news/a-brief-history-of-bloodletting.
40. Ibid.
41. Ibid.
42. Francesca Gould, *Why You Shouldn't Eat Your Boogers and Other Useless Information about Your Body* (Tarcher/Penguin, 2007).
43. www.history.com/news/a-brief-history-of-bloodletting.
44. www.pbs.org/wnet/nature/bloodysuckers/leech.html.
45. Francesca Gould, *Why You Shouldn't Eat Your Boogers and Other Useless Information about Your Body* (Tarcher/Penguin, 2007).

46. Ibid.
47. www.pbs.org/wnet/nature/bloodysuckers/leech.html.
48. Ibid.
49. www.economist.com/node/7001585.
50. Francesca Gould, *Why You Shouldn't Eat Your Boogers and Other Useless Information about Your Body* (Tarcher/Penguin, 2007).
51. www.princeton.edu/~paw/archive_new/PAW04-05/14-0511/features1 .html.
52. Ibid.
53. Ibid.
54. Francesca Gould, *Why You Shouldn't Eat Your Boogers and Other Useless Information about Your Body* (Tarcher/Penguin, 2007).
55. Joan Perkin, *Victorian Women* (New York University Press, 1995).
56. www.straightdope.com/columns/read/2465/what-is-nymphomania.
57. Carol Groneman, *Nymphomania: A History* (W. W. Norton, 2001).
58. Joan Perkin, *Victorian Women* (New York University Press, 1995).
59. Francesca Gould, *Why You Shouldn't Eat Your Boogers and Other Useless Information about Your Body* (Tarcher/Penguin, 2007).
60. Ibid.
61. Ibid.
62. Nathan Belofsky, *Strange Medicine: A Shocking History of Real Medical Practices Through the Ages* (Penguin, 2013).
63. Ibid.
64. Lucy Worsley, *If Walls Could Talk: An Intimate History of the Home* (Bloomsbury USA, 2012).
65. William Potts Dewees, *Treatise on the Physical and Medical Treatment of Children* (H. P. Carey & I. Lea, 1825).

3. THINGS THAT FALL FROM THE SKY

66. www.slate.com/articles/news_and_politics/explainer/2012/02/long_ island_couple_pelted_with_poo_where_do_airplanes_dump_their_waste_ .html.
67. Ibid.
68. Ibid.
69. Ibid.
70. http://old.post-gazette.com/neigh_north/20021121blueicenp3.asp.
71. www.foxnews.com/printer_friendly_wires/2006Oct20/0,4675,Aircraft ToiletIce,00.html.
72. http://gizmodo.com/5953877/what-happens-when-you-flush-a-toilet-on- an-airplane.
73. www.foxnews.com/science/2013/02/15/injuries-reported-after-meteorite- falls-in-russia-ural-mountains.
74. Ibid.
75. Ibid.
76. www.popularmechanics.com/science/environment/natural- disasters/4331114.
77. Ibid.

78. Ibid.
79. www.idph.state.il.us/public/hb/hbb&bdrp.htm.
80. Ibid.
81. Ibid.
82. Ibid.
83. www.wildlifedamagecontrol.net/birddroppings.php and www.idph.state
    .il.us/public/hb/hbb&bdrp.htm.
84. Ibid.
85. Ibid.
86. http://www.bbc.com/news/world-europe-20780780.
87. http://abcnews.go.com/blogs/headlines/2013/03/skydiver-craig-
    stapleton-survives-hitting-ground-at-30-mph.
88. www.popularmechanics.com/outdoors/survival/stories/4344037.
89. www.popularmechanics.com/science/environment/natural-
    disasters/4331114.
90. http://news.nationalgeographic.com/news/2011/01/110106-birds-falling-
    from-sky-bird-deaths-arkansas-science.
91. www.popularmechanics.com/science/environment/natural-
    disasters/4331114.
92. Ibid.
93. www.livescience.com/32170-can-it-really-rain-fish.html.
94. Ibid.
95. www.popularmechanics.com/science/environment/natural-
    disasters/4331114.
96. Ibid.
97. http://www.news.com.au/national/its-raining-fish-in-the-northern-
    territory-report/story-e6frfkvr-1225835295781.
98. www.cbsnews.com/8301-201_162-57541012/leopard-shark-falls-from-
    sky-onto-calif-golf-course.
99. www.wired.com/wiredscience/2013/02/thousands-of-spiders.
100. www.popularmechanics.com/science/environment/natural-
     disasters/4331114.
101. http://abcnews.go.com/blogs/headlines/2013/03/calif-girl-hit-with-2-
     foot-long-arrow-on-school-trip.
102. Ibid.
103. www.foxnews.com/story/0,2933,308676,00.html.
104. www.atlasobscura.com/articles/hail-no-an-account-of-the-worlds-biggest-
     deadliest-hailstorms.
105. Ibid.
106. www.guinnessworldrecords.com/world-records/3000/heaviest-hailstones.
107. www.guinnessworldrecords.com/world-records/11000/worst-hailstorm-
     disaster-death-toll.
108. http://science.nasa.gov/science-news/science-at-nasa/2008/19sep_pollen.
109. Ibid.
110. www.nytimes.com/2010/06/27/nyregion/27zoo.html?_r=0.
111. Ibid.
112. Ibid.
113. http://abclocal.go.com/wabc/story?section=news/local/new_
     york&id=9195124.

114. www.ncbi.nlm.nih.gov/pubmed/6502774.
115. Ibid.
116. http://blog.al.com/wire/2013/08/virginia_boy_7_dies_from_stray.html.
117. www.cdc.gov/mmwr/preview/mmwrhtml/mm5350a2.htm.
118. Ibid.
119. www.ucdmc.ucdavis.edu/vprp/publications/straybulletjtrauma.pdf.
120. www.washingtonpost.com/local/va-boy-7-dies-after-being-hit-by-stray-bullet-on-fourth-of-july/2013/07/05/5e555da0-e5de-11e2-80eb-3145e2994a55_story.html.
121. www.telegraph.co.uk/news/worldnews/northamerica/usa/6927917/Boy-killed-by-bullet-fired-three-miles-away.html.
122. www.theatlanticwire.com/national/2011/12/confirmed-firing-gun-air-can-kill-someone/46462.
123. www.bbc.co.uk/news/magazine-14616491.
124. Ibid.
125. Ibid.
126. Ibid.
127. www.ksat.com/news/man-says-plane-part-fell-into-backyard/-/478452/21163344/-/42rp87z/-/index.html.
128. http://abcnews.go.com/US/refrigerator-size-plane-door-crashes-washington-neighborhood/story?id=17194380.
129. www.nbcnewyork.com/news/local/Falling-Metal-Object-Long-Island-Aviation-Documents-Mystery-213433311.html.
130. http://environment.nationalgeographic.com/environment/global-warming/acid-rain-overview.
131. Ibid.
132. Ibid.
133. Ibid.
134. http://serc.carleton.edu/NAGTWorkshops/health/case_studies/volcanic_ash.html.
135. www.cnn.com/2013/02/26/world/africa/egypt-balloon-deaths.
136. www.theguardian.com/uk/2013/apr/25/man-street-stowaway-fell-plane.
137. www.independent.co.uk/news/uk/home-news/4000-mile-journey-ends-at-a-london-cemetery-jet-stowaway-probably-still-alive-when-he-fell-from-undercarriage-as-it-approached-heathrow-8587632.html.
138. www.dailymail.co.uk/news/article-2157266/Florida-plane-crash-Body-Boston-Bramlage-13-discovered-falling-plane-crashed.html.
139. www.dailymail.co.uk/news/article-2308614/Frozen-turkey-vulture-falls-sky-wings-iced-blizzard.html.

4. ALLEGED ALIEN ABDUCTIONS

140. http://thefw.com/famous-alien-abductions.
141. Ibid.
142. http://thefw.com/famous-alien-abductions; Chris A. Rutkowski, *The Big Book of UFOs* (Dundurn, 2010).
143. Chris A. Rutkowski, *The Big Book of UFOs* (Dundurn, 2010).
144. Ibid.

145. www.huffingtonpost.com/2013/09/11/48-percent-of-americans-believe-in-ufos_n_3900669.html.

146. www.livescience.com/20250-alien-abductions-origins.html.

147. http://thefw.com/famous-alien-abductions.

148. Ibid.

149. Ibid.

150. Ibid.

151. Book Sales, Inc., *The World's Greatest Alien Abduction Mysteries* (Book Sales, 2002).

152. http://thefw.com/famous-alien-abductions; Book Sales, Inc., *The World's Greatest Alien Abduction Mysteries* (Book Sales, 2002).

153. Book Sales, Inc., *The World's Greatest Alien Abduction Mysteries* (Book Sales, 2002).

154. Ibid.

155. http://thefw.com/famous-alien-abductions.

156. http://thefw.com/famous-alien-abductions; Book Sales, Inc., *The World's Greatest Alien Abduction Mysteries* (Book Sales, 2002).

157. http://science.howstuffworks.com/space/aliens-ufos/alien-abduction.htm.

158. Ibid.

159. http://thefw.com/famous-alien-abductions.

160. Chris A. Rutkowski, *The Big Book of UFOs* (Dundurn, 2010).

161. Book Sales, Inc., *The World's Greatest Alien Abduction Mysteries* (Book Sales, 2002).

162. http://ufos.about.com/od/aliensalienabduction/a/godfreyabducted.htm.

163. Ibid.

164. www.huffingtonpost.com/2013/09/11/48-percent-of-americans-believe-in-ufos_n_3900669.html.

165. Ibid.

166. Book Sales, Inc., *The World's Greatest Alien Abduction Mysteries* (Book Sales, 2002).

167. Daniel W. Fry and Rolf Telano, *The White Sands Incident* (Horus House Press, 1992).

168. Ibid.

169. Book Sales, Inc., *The World's Greatest Alien Abduction Mysteries* (Book Sales, 2002).

170. Ibid.

171. www.news.harvard.edu/gazette/2005/09.22/11-alien.html.

172. Ibid.

173. https://petitions.whitehouse.gov/response/searching-et-no-evidence-yet.

5. DISGUSTING FOOD FROM AROUND THE WORLD

174. http://travel.ca.msn.com/international/photogallery.aspx?cp-documentid=23957391&page=14.

175. http://mentalfloss.com/article/20523/casu-marzu-maggot-cheese-mediterranean.

176. www.gadling.com/2011/03/16/bizarre-foods-european-delicacies-by-country.

177. www.foxnews.com/leisure/2012/07/23/gross-or-great-unexpected-delicacies-from-around-world.
178. Ibid.
179. www.gadling.com/2011/03/16/bizarre-foods-european-delicacies-by-country.
180. www.foodnetwork.com/recipes/alton-brown/haggis-recipe.html.
181. www.epicurious.com/recipes/food/views/Black-Pudding-51145600.
182. www.gadling.com/2011/03/16/bizarre-foods-european-delicacies-by-country.
183. www.foxnews.com/leisure/2012/07/23/gross-or-great-unexpected-delicacies-from-around-world.
184. www.gadling.com/2011/03/16/bizarre-foods-european-delicacies-by-country.
185. www.tabletmag.com/jewish-life-and-religion/97599/a-disappearing-delicacy.
186. www.gadling.com/2011/03/16/bizarre-foods-european-delicacies-by-country.
187. www.kalofagas.ca.
188. http://listverse.com/2009/07/22/10-more-utterly-disgusting-foods.
189. Ibid.
190. http://news.bbc.co.uk/2/hi/europe/4867024.stm.
191. www.mongolfood.info/en/recipes/airag.html.
192. http://listverse.com/2009/07/22/10-more-utterly-disgusting-foods.
193. Ibid.
194. Ibid.
195. www.businessinsider.com/extreme-foods-from-around-the-world-2013-6?op=1.
196. www.huffingtonpost.com/2010/04/27/huitlacoche-corn-smut-goo_n_553422.html.
197. http://mentalfloss.com/article/20523/casu-marzu-maggot-cheese-mediterranean.
198. Ibid.
199. www.smithsonianmag.com/people-places/Scandinavians-Strange-Holiday-Lutefisk-Tradition.html.
200. www.nbcnews.com/id/18494880/%22%20%5Cl%20%22.UhUilJKsiSo.
201. www.culinaryschools.org/cuisine/10-disgusting-delicacies.
202. http://list25.com/25-of-the-strangest-foods-from-around-the-world.
203. www.gadling.com/2011/03/16/bizarre-foods-european-delicacies-by-country.
204. www.culinaryschools.org/cuisine/10-disgusting-delicacies.
205. Ibid.
206. www.foxnews.com/leisure/2012/07/23/gross-or-great-unexpected-delicacies-from-around-world.
207. http://list25.com/25-of-the-strangest-foods-from-around-the-world.
208. http://goafrica.about.com/od/botswana/ss/Mopane-Worm.htm.
209. www.simonseeks.com/blog/world%E2%80%99s-strangest-delicacies.
210. http://list25.com/25-of-the-strangest-foods-from-around-the-world.
211. Ibid.

212. www.foxnews.com/leisure/2012/07/23/gross-or-great-unexpected-delicacies-from-around-world.
213. Ibid.
214. Ibid.
215. www.theguardian.com/lifeandstyle/wordofmouth/2013/apr/16/camel-meat-one-hump-two.
216. Ibid.
217. Ibid.
218. www.thedailymeal.com/gross-or-great-27-unexpected-delicacies-around-world-slideshow.
219. Ibid.
220. www.huffingtonpost.com/2013/05/08/interesting-food-in-the-world_n_3239963.html.
221. www.popcrunch.com/12-of-the-most-disgusting-delicacies.
222. Ibid.
223. www.businessinsider.com/extreme-foods-from-around-the-world-2013-6?op=1.
224. Ibid.
225. www.independenttraveler.com/travel-tips/funny-travel/seven-strange-foods-from-around-the-world.
226. www.businessinsider.com/extreme-foods-from-around-the-world-2013-6?op=1.
227. http://listverse.com/2009/07/22/10-more-utterly-disgusting-foods.
228. www.foodandwine.com/articles/worlds-scariest-foods.
229. www.businessinsider.com/extreme-foods-from-around-the-world-2013-6?op=1.
230. www.independenttraveler.com/travel-tips/funny-travel/seven-strange-foods-from-around-the-world.

6. BOOGERS

231. www.urbandictionary.com/define.php?term=rhinotillexis.
232. www.urbandictionary.com/define.php?term=mucophagy.
233. www.vat19.com/brain-candy/booger-facts.cfm.
234. www.oprah.com/oprahshow/Dr-Oz-on-Health-and-Hygiene.
235. Francesca Gould, *Why You Shouldn't Eat Your Boogers and Other Useless Information about Your Body* (Tarcher/Penguin, 2007).
236. Jody Sullivan Rake, *Why Feet Smell and Other Gross Facts about Your Body*. (Capstone, 2012).
237. Ibid.
238. Francesca Gould, *Why You Shouldn't Eat Your Boogers and Other Useless Information about Your Body* (Tarcher/Penguin, 2007).
239. Ibid.
240. Ibid.
241. Ibid.
242. http://kidshealth.org/kid/talk/yucky/booger.html.
243. Ibid.
244. Ibid.

245. www.livestrong.com/article/290573-the-function-of-nose-hairs.
246. http://kidshealth.org/kid/talk/yucky/booger.html.
247. www.boogiewipes.com/booger-facts.
248. Ibid.
249. www.uamshealth.com/?id=12781&sid=1.
250. www.boogiewipes.com/booger-facts.
251. www.webmd.com/allergies/features/the-truth-about-mucus.
252. www.boogiewipes.com/booger-facts.
253. Ibid.
254. Ibid.
255. Jody Sullivan Rake, *Why Feet Smell and Other Gross Facts about Your Body*. (Capstone, 2012).
256. www.telegraph.co.uk/news/uknews/3566273/Man-dies-from-picking-his-nose.html.

7. STOOPID CRIMINALS

257. www.rd.com/slideshows/stupid-criminals-smart-technology.
258. www.rd.com/slideshows/dumb-criminals-worse-luck-than-you.
259. www.cnn.com/2008/WORLD/asiapcf/02/28/biker.meeting.
260. http://abclocal.go.com/ktrk/story?section=news/bizarre&id=5789597.
261. www.contracostatimes.com/news/ci_11627101.
262. www.shortlist.com/home/worlds-dumbest-criminals.
263. Ibid.
264. National Geographic, *Weird but True! Stupid Criminals* (National Geographic Children's Books, 2012).
265. Ibid.
266. Ibid.
267. www.guinnessworldrecords.com/world-records/3000/oldest-convicted-bank-robber.
268. Leland Gregory, *The Stupid Crook Book* (Andrews McMeel, 2002).
269. Ibid.
270. Ibid.
271. http://articles.latimes.com/1993-05-14/local/me-35384_1_serial-killer.
272. Gini Graham Scott, *The Robber Who Shot Himself in the Face* (Sourcebooks, 2009).
273. Ibid.
274. Ibid.
275. Ibid.
276. www.abc27.com/story/23627366/suspected-shoplifters-left-baby-behind-police-say.
277. http://abclocal.go.com/ktrk/story?section=news/bizarre&id=7358088.
278. www.foxnews.com/story/2008/05/01/texas-cops-bust-man-trying-to-cash-360-billion-check.
279. www.ocala.com/article/20130709/ARTICLES/130709720.
280. www.murfreesboropost.com/bizarre-drug-dealer-alerts-police-to-stolen-weed-cms-36511.
281. www.kpho.com/story/23105968/pd-man-who-stole-ambulance-fought-with-officers-spit-at-nurse.

282. www.10news.com/news/police-thieves-stole-jukebox-from-rancho-bernardo-hooters-thought-it-was-atm.
283. www.wltx.com/news/article/215828/2/Trail-of-Cheetos-Le.
284. http://ktla.com/2013/03/05/half-naked-dui-suspect-tries-to-flee-in-toy-truck/#axzz2jozTpGX2.
285. http://abcnews.go.com/US/LegalCenter/story?id=507964.

8. TORTURE DEVICES

286. John Lothrop Motley, *The Rise of the Dutch Republic* (Harper & Brothers, 1900).
287. Geoffrey Abbott, *What a Way to Go: The Guillotine, the Pendulum, the Thousand Cuts, the Spanish Donkey, and 66 Other Ways of Putting Someone to Death* (Macmillan, 2007).
288. Mark P. Donnelly and Daniel Diehl, *The Big Book of Pain: Torture & Punishment Through History* (History Publishing Group, 2011).
289. Ibid.
290. www.huffingtonpost.com/2012/12/13/deals-from-the-darkside-torture-tongs-video_n_2291320.html.
291. Ruth Scurr, *Fatal Purity: Robespierre and the French Revolution* (Macmillan, 2007).
292. www.crimelibrary.com/photogallery/cruel-and-unusual-punishment.html.
293. Ibid.
294. Ibid.
295. Ibid.
296. Ibid.
297. Ibid.
298. www.slate.com/articles/news_and_politics/jurisprudence/2006/05/take_my_life_please.html.
299. www.medievality.com/garrotte.html.
300. www.crimelibrary.com/photogallery/cruel-and-unusual-punishment.html.
301. http://antiwar.com/blog/2011/11/04/uzbek-dictator-shifts-from-boiling-people-to-freezing-them.
302. www.tribunesandtriumphs.org/colosseum/roman-executions-at-the-colosseum.htm.
303. www.trutv.com/library/crime/photogallery/cruel-and-unusual-punishment.html.
304. http://list25.com/25-of-humanitys-most-brutal-methods-of-execution.
305. Ibid.
306. Jean Kellaway, *The History of Torture and Execution: From Early Civilization Through Medieval Times to the Present* (Globe Pequot, 2002).
307. www.trutv.com/library/crime/photogallery/cruel-and-unusual-punishment.html.
308. Kenneth Allen, *The Story of Gunpowder* (Wayland, 1973).
309. www.thefreedictionary.com/gibbeting.
310. www.medievalwarfare.info/torture.htm#gibbet.
311. www.trutv.com/library/crime/photogallery/cruel-and-unusual-punishment.html.

312. http://history.howstuffworks.com/history-vs-myth/10-medieval-torture-devices1.htm.
313. http://listverse.com/2007/09/12/top-10-gruesome-methods-of-execution.
314. www.trutv.com/library/crime/photogallery/cruel-and-unusual-punishment.html.
315. www.tortureamsterdam.com/textpage/index/10.
316. www.medievalwarfare.info/torture.htm#judas.
317. Ibid.
318. Ibid.
319. Ibid.
320. www.trutv.com/library/crime/index.html.
321. http://www.crimelibrary.com/photogallery/cruel-and-unusual-punishment.html.
322. www.medievalwarfare.info/torture.htm#thumbscrews.
323. http://history.howstuffworks.com/history-vs-myth/10-medieval-torture-devices10.htm.
324. Ibid.
325. www.medievality.com/the-rack-torture.html.
326. Ibid.
327. www.medievality.com/flaying-torture.html.
328. Ibid.
329. http://listverse.com/2010/07/18/10-additional-gruesome-torture-devices.
330. www.medievality.com/spanish-spider.html.
331. Christine Mason Sutherland and Rebecca Jane Sutcliffe, *The Changing Tradition: Women in the History of Rhetoric* (University of Calgary Press, 1999).
332. Ibid.
333. www.medievality.com/toe-wedging.html.
334. Ibid.
335. www.medievality.com/copper-boot.html.
336. Ibid.
337. www.environmentalgraffiti.com/featured/most-horrific-russian-torture-devices/8850?image=3; http://history.howstuffworks.com/history-vs-myth/10-medieval-torture-devices1.htm.
338. www.environmentalgraffiti.com/featured/most-horrific-russian-torture-devices/8850?image=3; http://history.howstuffworks.com/history-vs-myth/10-medieval-torture-devices1.htm.
339. http://www.medievality.com/street-sweepers-daughter.html.

9. PUBLIC BATHROOMS

340. http://news.cnet.com/8301-17852_3-20081595-71/study-19-percent-of-people-drop-phones-down-toilet.
341. www.cnn.com/2008/HEALTH/10/03/bathroom.hygiene.
342. Ibid.
343. www.huffingtonpost.com/uloop/public-restroom_b_1389988.html.
344. http://abcnews.go.com/Entertainment/WolfFiles/story?id=93103.
345. Ibid.

346. www.scientificamerican.com/article.cfm?id=pitfalls-of-inventing-a-better-toilet&page=2.
347. http://news.cnet.com/8301-17852_3-20028100-71.html.
348. www.medieval-castles.net/castle_architecture/garderobes.htm.
349. www.buzzfeed.com/briangalindo/15-truly-bizarre-facts-about-ancient-rome.
350. www.businessinsider.com/absurd-laws-of-singapore-2012-6.
351. Ibid.
352. www.today.com/id/21423163/ns/today-today_health/t/soap-germiest-places-your-life/#.UrNvE41RbPM.
353. www.huffingtonpost.com/2011/12/20/cocaine-found-baby-changing-tables_n_1160176.html.
354. mentalfloss.com/article/23210/toilet-paper-history-how-america-convinced-world-wipe.
355. www.nytimes.com/1998/08/21/nyregion/guilty-plea-by-mother-20-in-prom-death.html?pagewanted=all.
356. www.snopes.com/military/pentagonbathrooms.asp.
357. www.webmd.com/balance/features/what-can-you-catch-in-restrooms.
358. Ibid.
359. Ibid.
360. Ibid.
361. Ibid.
362. http://listverse.com/2009/09/04/top-15-facts-you-probably-dont-know.

10. LIES, LIARS, AND FRAUDS

363. http://newswatch.nationalgeographic.com/2012/12/06/liar-liar-nose-on-fire.
364. www.news.cornell.edu/stories/2010/12/people-lie-way-manage-modern-communications.
365. www.onthemedia.org/story/131287-the-face-never-lies/transcript.
366. Ibid.
367. www.psychologicalscience.org/index.php/news/releases/when-do-we-lie-when-were-short-on-time-and-long-on-reasons.html.
368. http://usatoday30.usatoday.com/news/health/story/2012-08-04/honesty-beneficial-to-health/56782648/1.
369. Ibid.
370. www.businessinsider.com/these-subsets-of-americans-are-most-likely-to-lie-on-their-resumes-2012-5.
371. http://chronicle.com/blogs/percolator/the-trustworthiness-of-beards/22581.
372. www.legalaffairs.org/issues/November-December-2002/review_koerner_novdec2002.msp.
373. www.livescience.com/10574-robots-learn-lie.html.
374. www.history.com/this-day-in-history/rosie-ruiz-fakes-boston-marathon-win.
375. Ibid.
376. http://blogs.smithsonianmag.com/history/2012/08/the-smoothest-con-man-that-ever-lived.

377. http://content.time.com/time/specials/packages
/article/0,28804,1900621_1900618_1900620,00.html.
378. www.bbc.co.uk/legacies/myths_legends/england/bristol/article_1.shtml.
379. www.slate.com/articles/arts/tangled_web/2002/10/the_nigerian_
nightmare.html.
380. www.nytimes.com/2004/02/27/nyregion/27BUTT.html?ex=1393218000.
381. http://archive.archaeology.org/online/features/hoaxes/beringer.html.
382. www.trutv.com/library/crime/criminal_mind/scams/frank_abagnale
/index.html.
383. Ibid.
384. http://content.time.com/time/specials/packages
/article/0,28804,1931133_1931132_1931123,00.html.
385. www.theglobeandmail.com/life/health-and-fitness/medical-fraud-revealed-
in-discredited-vaccine-autism-study/article621543.
386. www.neatorama.com/2006/09/19/10scientific-frauds-that-rocked-the-
world/#!rqSLs.
387. www.museumofhoaxes.com/hoax/archive/permalink/the_cardiff_giant.
388. www.neatorama.com/2006/09/19/10scientific-frauds-that-rocked-the-
world/#!rqSLs.
389. www.bbc.co.uk/history/ancient/archaeology/piltdown_man_01.shtml.
390. http://sports.espn.go.com/oly/columns/story?id=2039471.
391. Ibid.
392. http://money.cnn.com/2009/04/24/news/newsmakers/madoff.fortune.
393. www.npr.org/templates/story/story.php?storyId=124208012.
394. www.cleveland.com/metro/index.ssf/2012/06/ohios_amish_bernie_
madoff_gets.html.
395. www.globalsecurity.org/military/world/war/albania.htm.
396. www.smithsonianmag.com/people-places/In-Ponzi-We-Trust.html.
397. www.today.com/id/23473811#.UsoVwvZRbPM.

11. BIRTH CONTROL

398. Autumn Stanley, *Mothers and Daughters of Invention: Notes for a Revised
History of Technology* (Rutgers University Press, 1995).
399. Vern LeRoy Bullough and Bonnie Bullough, eds., *Human Sexuality: An
Encyclopedia* (Routledge, 1994).
400. http://catholiceducation.org/articles/religion/re0663.html.
401. www.afn.org/~afn32612/Contraception.htm.
402. www.health.com/health/gallery/0,20306647_4,00.html.
403. Ibid.
404. http://en.bab.la/dictionary/german-english/antibabypille.
405. http://guildofscientifictroubadours.com/2007/07/21/baboon-birth-
control.
406. www.medicinenet.com/script/main/art.asp?articlekey=52188.
407. Ibid.
408. Ibid.
409. http://content.time.com/time/magazine/article/0,9171,1983970,00.html.
410. http://thesocietypages.org/socimages/2013/09/27/the-secret-of-vintage-
lysol-douche-ads.

411. www.abc.net.au/news/2003-08-13/toronto-museum-explores-history-of-contraceptives/1463884.
412. Ibid.
413. www.plannedparenthood.org/resources/research-papers/history-birth-control-methods-26784.htm.
414. www.nytimes.com/1994/03/08/science/in-ancient-times-flowers-and-fennel-for-family-planning.html.
415. Ibid.
416. www.sciencemuseum.org.uk/broughttolife/themes/birthanddeath/condom.aspx.
417. Ibid.

12. MENTAL MONARCHS

418. www.biography.com/people/caligula-9235253.
419. Ibid.
420. Frank N. Magill, *The Ancient World: Dictionary of World Biography*, vol. 1 (Routledge, 2003).
421. www.pbs.org/empires/romans/empire/caligula.html.
422. www.biography.com/people/caligula-9235253.
423. www.livescience.com/40277-emperor-nero-facts.html.
424. www.biography.com/people/nero-9421713.
425. Michael Farquhar, *A Treasury of Royal Scandals* (Penguin, 2001).
426. Ibid.
427. Ibid.
428. Vasily Rudich, *Political Dissidence under Nero: The Price of Dissimulation* (Psychology Press, 1993).
429. Michael Farquhar, *A Treasury of Royal Scandals* (Penguin, 2001).
430. www.biography.com/people/nero-9421713.
431. Michael Farquhar, *A Treasury of Royal Scandals* (Penguin, 2001).
432. www.cracked.com/article_20170_the-5-most-hilariously-insane-rulers-all-time.html.
433. Ibid.
434. Francesca Gould, *Why You Shouldn't Eat Your Boogers and Other Useless Information about Your Body* (Tarcher/Penguin, 2007).
435. http://mentalfloss.com/article/12508/11-monarchs-who-went-insane.
436. Francesca Gould, *Why You Shouldn't Eat Your Boogers and Other Useless Information about Your Body* (Tarcher/Penguin, 2007).
437. Ibid.
438. http://news.discovery.com/history/archaeology/henry-viii-blood-disorder-110311.htm.
439. Ibid.
440. http://www.biography.com/people/ivan-the-terrible-9350679.
441. Ibid.
442. http://europeanhistory.about.com/library/weekly/aa042701b.htm.
443. www.biography.com/people/ivan-the-terrible-9350679.
444. Ibid.
445. http://mentalfloss.com/article/12508/11-monarchs-who-went-insane.

446. Ibid.
447. Ulf Johansson, *DK Eyewitness Travel Guide: Sweden* (Penguin, 2011).
448. http://mentalfloss.com/article/12508/11-monarchs-who-went-insane.
449. Ibid.
450. http://content.time.com/time/specials/packages /article/0,28804,2030145_2030165_2030173,00.html.
451. Ibid.
452. www.history.org/Foundation/journal/Spring10/king.cfm.
453. Ibid.
454. Michael Farquhar, *A Treasury of Royal Scandals* (Penguin, 2001).
455. www.history.org/Foundation/journal/Spring10/king.cfm.
456. Michael Farquhar, *A Treasury of Royal Scandals* (Penguin, 2001).
457. www.cracked.com/article_20170_the-5-most-hilariously-insane-rulers-all-time.html.
458. Ibid.
459. http://mentalfloss.com/article/12508/11-monarchs-who-went-insane.
460. Ibid.
461. Ibid.
462. www.theatlantic.com/infocus/2011/06/the-125th-anniversary-of-the-death-of-king-ludwig-ii/100085.
463. Ibid.
464. Francesca Gould, *Why You Shouldn't Eat Your Boogers and Other Useless Information about Your Body* (Tarcher/Penguin, 2007).
465. www.cracked.com/article_20170_the-5-most-hilariously-insane-rulers-all-time.html.
466. David Hebditch and Ken Connor, *How to Stage a Military Coup: From Planning to Execution* (Skyhorse Publishing, 2009).
467. www.cracked.com/article_20170_the-5-most-hilariously-insane-rulers-all-time.html.
468. Ibid.

13. CREEPY CRAWLIES

469. www.cdc.gov/parasites/scabies/.
470. Ibid.
471. Ibid.
472. Francesca Gould, *Why You Shouldn't Eat Your Boogers and Other Useless Information about Your Body* (Tarcher/Penguin, 2007).
473. Ibid.
474. www.orkin.com/cockroaches.
475. Ibid.
476. www.pestworldforkids.org/pest-guide/cockroaches.
477. www.cdc.gov/parasites/bedbugs.
478. Ibid.
479. www.cdc.gov/mold/faqs.htm.
480. www.medicinenet.com/objects_or_insects_in_ear/article.htm#objects_or_insects_in_ear_overview.
481. http://news.bbc.co.uk/cbbcnews/hi/uk/newsid_3109000/3109536.stm.

482. Francesca Gould, *Why You Shouldn't Eat Your Boogers and Other Useless Information about Your Body* (Tarcher/Penguin, 2007).
483. Ibid.
484. Ibid.
485. www.cdc.gov/parasites/naegleria.
486. www.webmd.com/brain/brain-eating-amoeba.
487. Ibid.
488. www.cdc.gov/parasites/naegleria.
489. Ibid.
490. http://science.discovery.com/creatures/10-bizarre-rat-facts.htm.
491. Ibid.
492. www.ratbehavior.org/WhatIsMyRatDoingFAQ.htm#Infanticide.
493. http://science.discovery.com/creatures/10-bizarre-rat-facts.htm.
494. www.ratbehavior.org/Teeth.htm.
495. http://science.discovery.com/creatures/10-bizarre-rat-facts.htm.
496. Ibid.
497. www.afrma.org/brdstf_inbreeding.htm.

14. COLOSSAL BLUNDERS

498. www.npr.org/templates/story/story.php?storyId=106637066.
499. http://consumerist.com/2007/05/07/new-jersey-comcast-shows-porn-instead-of-disney-channel.
500. www.washingtonpost.com/wp-srv/inatl/longterm/coldwar/shatter031598a.htm.
501. http://skywalk.kansascity.com/articles/20-years-later-fatal-disaster-remains-impossible-forget.
502. www.nps.gov/linc/historyculture/lincoln-memorial-myths.htm.
503. www.nytimes.com/1987/06/11/us/after-3-centuries-a-student-figures-that-newton-erred.html.
504. www.wired.com/thisdayintech/2010/11/1110mars-climate-observer-report.
505. www.chicagotribune.com/news/politics/chi-chicagodays-eastlanddisaster-story,0,5718377.story.
506. www.americanheritage.com/content/calumet-tragedy.
507. http://usatoday30.usatoday.com/news/nation/2007-02-17-florida-reef_x.htm.
508. www.spiegel.de/international/zeitgeist/a-quarter-century-after-chernobyl-radioactive-boar-on-the-rise-in-germany-a-709345.html.
509. http://aviation-safety.net/database/record.php?id=19710730-1.
510. http://content.time.com/time/health/article/0,8599,1578074,00.html.
511. http://articles.latimes.com/1992-04-27/news/mn-630_1_sewer-system.
512. www.cbc.ca/halifaxexplosion/he2_ruins/he2_ruins_explosion.html.
513. www.wsdot.wa.gov/tnbhistory/default.htm.

15. PARENTING: YOU'RE DOING IT WRONG

514. www.whsv.com/news/headlines/Mother-Responds-to-Controversy-After-Son-Dresses-as-Klansman-for-Halloween—230306501.html.

515. www.dailymail.co.uk/news/article-2491454/Mom-arrested-letting-year-old-drive-year-old-passenger.html.
516. http://chicago.cbslocal.com/2013/10/21/two-arrested-in-brawl-over-prize-tickets-at-chuck-e-cheese.
517. www.seattlepi.com/local/article/Charge-Dad-tried-to-kill-son-4-with-heroin-on-4852931.php.
518. www.reviewjournal.com/news/crime-courts/mom-behind-payments-when-11-year-old-set-fire-minivan.
519. www.huffingtonpost.com/2013/09/03/breastfeeding-on-moped_n_3860757.html.
520. www.cnn.com/2013/12/11/us/texas-teen-dwi-wreck.
521. http://157.166.224.196/documents/mother-daughter-take-topless-photo-675423.
522. http://157.166.224.196/buster/mom-encourages-daughters-fight-874312.
523. http://157.166.224.196/buster/mom-bites-daughters-breast-678543.
524. http://157.166.255.196/documents/grandma-steals-teachers-wallet-786543.
525. http://seattle.cbslocal.com/2013/04/01/easter-egg-hunt-at-seattle-zoo-turns-violent.
526. www.parenting.com/blogs/show-and-tell/elina-parenting/ugly-baby.
527. www.parenting.com/blogs/show-and-tell/elina-parenting/mother-gives-toddler-beer.
528. www.crimelibrary.com/blog/2013/10/03/police-baby-sitting-grandma-got-drunk-in-street-tried-to-give-away-grandchild/index.html.
529. www.cbsnews.com/news/okla-woman-tries-to-sell-children-on-facebook-to-get-bail-money-for-boyfriend-police-say.
530. www.parenting.com/blogs/show-and-tell/filip-parentingcom/deadbeat.

16. AMUSEMENT PARK ACCIDENTS

531. http://vitals.nbcnews.com/_news/2013/05/01/17988578-amusement-rides-hurt-4400-kids-a-year-large-study-finds?lite.
532. Ibid.
533. Virginia Sole-Smith, "Roller Coaster Roulette," *Good Housekeeping*, June 2008, pp. 146–203.
534. http://vitals.nbcnews.com/_news/2013/05/01/17988578-amusement-rides-hurt-4400-kids-a-year-large-study-finds?lite.
535. Ibid.
536. Virginia Sole-Smith, "Roller Coaster Roulette," *Good Housekeeping*, June 2008, pp. 146–203.
537. Ibid.
538. www.iaapa.org/safety-and-advocacy/safety/amusement-ride-safety/regulations-standards.
539. Ibid.
540. Marc Silver, Sara Hammel, Linda Kulman, Marissa Melton, Holly J. Morris, Joellen Posey, Kenneth Terrell, and Mike Tharp, "Fatal Attractions," *U.S. News & World Report*, September 13, 1999, p. 56.
541. Ibid.
542. Ibid.

543. www.macleans.ca/news/world/death-on-a-roller-coaster.
544. Marc Silver, Sara Hammel, Linda Kulman, Marissa Melton, Holly J. Morris, Joellen Posey, Kenneth Terrell, and Mike Tharp, "Fatal Attractions," *U.S. News & World Report*, September 13, 1999, p. 56.
545. www.rideaccidents.com.
546. Virginia Sole-Smith, "Roller Coaster Roulette," *Good Housekeeping*, June 2008, pp. 146–203; http://www.ocregister.com/news/changes-143726-disneyland-orange.html.
547. Marc Silver, Sara Hammel, Linda Kulman, Marissa Melton, Holly J. Morris, Joellen Posey, Kenneth Terrell, and Mike Tharp, "Fatal Attractions," *U.S. News & World Report*, September 13, 1999, p. 56.
548. www.dallasnews.com/news/community-news/best-southwest/headlines/20130723-tarrant-medical-examiner-reports-on-six-flags-roller-coaster-fatality.ece; http://www.inquisitr.com/863579/rosy-esparza-mother-who-fell-off-roller-coaster-was-on-first-ever-trip-to-six-flags.
549. http://blogs.dallasobserver.com/unfairpark/2013/09/texas_giant_reopen_lawsuit.php.
550. Ibid.
551. Virginia Sole-Smith, "Roller Coaster Roulette," *Good Housekeeping*, June 2008, pp. 146–203.
552. http://www.macleans.ca/news/world/death-on-a-roller-coaster.
553. http://www.8newsnow.com/story/3235748/stratospheres-newest-ride-malfunctions.
554. http://seattletimes.com/html/nationworld/2002335542_webepcot14.html.
555. www.space.com/2292-woman-dies-riding-disney-mission-space.html.
556. http://www.nytimes.com/1999/08/30/nyregion/roller-coaster-hurtles-wrong-way-killing-2.html.
557. Ibid.
558. www.rideaccidents.com.
559. Ibid.
560. www.freerepublic.com/focus/f-news/944401/posts.
561. www.rideaccidents.com.
562. Ibid.
563. www.mandatory.com/2012/06/20/the-10-worst-roller-coaster-disasters/2.
564. www.rideaccidents.com.
565. Ibid.
566. www.orlandosentinel.com/news/local/breakingnews/orl-deaths-at-walt-disney-world,0,7863626.htmlstory.
567. Ibid.
568. Ibid.
569. http://articles.latimes.com/2001/sep/23/local/me-48925.
570. www.rideaccidents.com/rides.html.
571. www.rideaccidents.com/1998.html#apr18.
572. www.mandatory.com/2012/06/20/the-10-worst-roller-coaster-disasters/2.
573. Ibid.
574. www.wtae.com/news/national/-/9681152/21096742/-/ew76mp/-/index.html.

575. www.nytimes.com/1991/06/11/us/3-killed-at-amusement-park.html.

17. ISOLATED PLACES

576. http://japan.apike.ca/japan_okunoshima.html.
577. www.damninteresting.com/the-smoldering-ruins-of-centralia.
578. Ibid.
579. www.telegraph.co.uk/news/worldnews/asia/india/1509987/Stone-Age-tribe-kills-fishermen-who-strayed-on-to-island.html.
580. Ibid.
581. www.atlasobscura.com/places/the-crystal-maiden-of-the-actun-tunichil-muknal-cave.
582. Ibid.
583. www.atlasobscura.com/places/telegraph-island-jazirat-al-maqlab.
584. http://adventure.howstuffworks.com/most-remote-place.htm.
585. Ibid.
586. www.atlasobscura.com/places/southern-pole-of-inaccessibility.
587. www.cntraveler.com/daily-traveler/2013/04/tree-of-tenere-niger-africa-maphead-ken-jennings.
588. www.atlasobscura.com/articles/essential-guide-to-bars-at-the-end-of-the-world.
589. www.atlasobscura.com/places/tristan-da-cunha; http://adventure.howstuffworks.com/most-remote-place.htm.
590. Ibid.
591. www.doc.govt.nz/conservation/historic/by-region/southland/subantarctic-islands/antipodes-island-castaway-depot.
592. http://blogs.smithsonianmag.com/smartnews/2012/11/there-are-over-200-bodies-on-mount-everest-and-theyre-used-as-landmarks.
593. http://www.bbc.co.uk/news/world-asia-pacific-16340072.
594. http://articles.chicagotribune.com/2001-08-12/travel/0108110002_1_peach-springs-havasupai-indians-south-rim.
595. www.biology-online.org/articles/atacama_rover_helps_nasa.html.
596. www.foxnews.com/travel/2013/10/23/worlds-most-remote-locations.
597. Ibid.
598. Ibid.
599. www.smithsonianmag.com/history/for-40-years-this-russian-family-was-cut-off-from-all-human-contact-unaware-of-world-war-ii-7354256/?no-ist.
600. www.foxnews.com/travel/2013/10/23/worlds-most-remote-locations.
601. www.greenland.com/en/explore-greenland/oestgroenland/ittoqqortoormiit.aspx.
602. http://education.nationalgeographic.com/education/encyclopedia/south-pole/?ar_a=1.
603. www.hashima-island.co.uk.
604. Ibid.
605. Ibid.
606. Ibid.

18. CRYPTIDS: OR CREATURES YOU DON'T WANT TO BELIEVE EXIST

607. Loren Coleman, *Crytozoology A to Z* (Fireside, 1999).
608. Ibid.
609. Ibid.
610. http://science.howstuffworks.com/science-vs-myth/strange-creatures/bigfoot.htm.
611. Ibid.
612. Kelly Milner Halls, Rick Spears, and Roxyanne Young, *Tales of the Cryptids* (Darby Creek, 2006).
613. http://science.howstuffworks.com/science-vs-myth/strange-creatures/bigfoot.htm.
614. Ibid.
615. www.history.com/this-day-in-history/loch-ness-monster-sighted.
616. Ibid.
617. Ibid.
618. Ibid.
619. http://news.discovery.com/animals/endangered-species/famous-cryptids-loch-ness-monster-110719.htm.
620. www.pantheon.org/articles/y/yeti.html.
621. Loren Coleman, *Crytozoology A to Z* (Fireside, 1999).
622. Ibid.
623. www.pantheon.org/articles/y/yeti.html.
624. Kelly Milner Halls, Rick Spears, and Roxyanne Young, *Tales of the Cryptids* (Darby Creek, 2006).
625. www.environmentalgraffiti.com/news-cryptids-more-terrifying-mongolian-death-worm.
626. Ibid.
627. www.bfro.net/news/GoodallTranscript.asp.
628. http://news.discovery.com/animals/pets/chupacabra-mystery-solved.htm; http://news.nationalgeographic.com/news/2010/10/101028-chupacabra-evolution-halloween-science-monsters-chupacabras-picture.
629. http://news.discovery.com/animals/pets/chupacabra-mystery-solved.htm.
630. Ibid.
631. http://news.nationalgeographic.com/news/2010/10/101028-chupacabra-evolution-halloween-science-monsters-chupacabras-picture.
632. www.environmentalgraffiti.com/bizarre/news-legacy-mothman; http://animal.discovery.com/tv-shows/lost-tapes/creatures/mothman.htm.
633. www.environmentalgraffiti.com/bizarre/news-legacy-mothman.
634. http://animal.discovery.com/tv-shows/lost-tapes/creatures/mothman.htm.
635. http://www.environmentalgraffiti.com/bizarre/news-legacy-mothman; http://animal.discovery.com/tv-shows/lost-tapes/creatures/mothman.htm.
636. Mark Turner, "Couples See Man-Sized Bird . . . Creature . . . Something," *Point Pleasant* (West Virginia) *Register*, November 18, 1966.
637. http://animal.discovery.com/tv-shows/lost-tapes/creatures/mothman.htm.
638. Ibid.

639. Deena West Budd, *The Weiser Field Guide to Cryptozoology* (Red Wheel/
     Weiser, 2010).
640. Loren Coleman, *Crytozoology A to Z* (Fireside, 1999).
641. www.environmentalgraffiti.com/news-cryptids-more-terrifying-
     mongolian-death-worm.
642. Ibid.
643. Ibid.
644. Loren Coleman, *Crytozoology A to Z* (Fireside, 1999).
645. Deena West Budd, *The Weiser Field Guide to Cryptozoology* (Red Wheel/
     Weiser, 2010).
646. http://news.discovery.com/animals/endangered-species/famous-cryptids-
     loch-ness-monster-110719.htm.
647. Ibid.
648. Kelly Milner Halls, Rick Spears, and Roxyanne Young, *Tales of the Cryptids*
     (Darby Creek, 2006).
649. www.csicop.org/si/show/measure_of_a_monster_investigating_the_
     champ_photo.
650. Loren Coleman, *Crytozoology A to Z* (Fireside, 1999).
651. Deena West Budd, *The Weiser Field Guide to Cryptozoology* (Red Wheel/
     Weiser, 2010).
652. Ibid.
653. Loren Coleman, *Crytozoology A to Z* (Fireside, 1999).
654. Ibid.
655. Deena West Budd, *The Weiser Field Guide to Cryptozoology* (Red Wheel/
     Weiser, 2010); Loren Coleman, *Crytozoology A to Z* (Fireside, 1999).
656. www.environmentalgraffiti.com/news-cryptids-more-terrifying-
     mongolian-death-worm.
657. www.cryptomundo.com/cryptozoo-news/akkorokamui; www
     .environmentalgraffiti.com/news-cryptids-more-terrifying-mongolian-
     death-worm.
658. www.environmentalgraffiti.com/news-cryptids-more-terrifying-
     mongolian-death-worm.
659. Kelly Milner Halls, Rick Spears, and Roxyanne Young, *Tales of the Cryptids*
     (Darby Creek, 2006).
660. www.yowiehunters.com.au/index.php/northern-territory.
661. Loren Coleman, *Crytozoology A to Z* (Fireside, 1999).
662. Deena West Budd, *The Weiser Field Guide to Cryptozoology* (Red Wheel/
     Weiser, 2010).
663. Ibid.
664. Ibid.
665. www.syfy.com/destinationtruth/episodes/season/2/episode/210/ahool_
     and_pinatubo.
666. Deena West Budd, *The Weiser Field Guide to Cryptozoology* (Red Wheel/
     Weiser, 2010).
667. Ibid.
668. Ibid.

19. FOOD FAILS

669. http://eatthis.menshealth.com/slideshow/20-scariest-food-facts.
670. well.blogs.nytimes.com/2007/12/05/a-high-price-for-healthy-food.
671. http://eatthis.menshealth.com/slideshow/20-scariest-food-facts.
672. www.breastcancerfund.org/clear-science/radiation-chemicals-and-breast-cancer/bovine-growth-hormone.html.
673. http://eatthis.menshealth.com/slideshow/20-scariest-food-facts.
674. Ibid.
675. www.nytimes.com/2009/12/31/us/31meat.html?pagewanted=all&_r=0.
676. http://mentalfloss.com/article/29133/how-much-rodent-filth-does-fda-allow.
677. Ibid.
678. Ibid.
679. http://www.fda.gov/food/guidanceregulation/guidancedocumentsregulatoryinformation/ucm056174.htm.
680. Ibid.
681. Ibid.
682. Ibid.
683. http://mentalfloss.com/article/29133/how-much-rodent-filth-does-fda-allow.
684. www.sheknows.com/food-and-recipes/articles/845051/the-top-ten-scariest-food-facts.
685. Ibid.
686. www.businessinsider.com/amazing-facts-mcdonalds-2010-12?op=1.
687. Ibid.
688. Ibid.
689. Ibid.
690. http://positivemed.com/2013/04/20/10-disgusting-facts-about-fast-food.
691. Ibid.
692. www.wisegeek.com/what-is-propylene-glycol-alginate.htm.
693. http://positivemed.com/2013/04/20/10-disgusting-facts-about-fast-food.
694. www.businessinsider.com/castoreum-used-in-food-and-perfume-2013-10.
695. http://health.yahoo.net/experts/menshealth/12-scariest-things-your-food.
696. http://online.wsj.com/news/articles/SB10001424052748703834804576300991196803916.
697. www.peta.org/about/faq/Are-animal-ingredients-included-in-white-sugar.aspx.

20. DRIVERS WHO SUCK

698. "Texting While Driving Now Surpasses Drinking and Driving for Teenage Accidents and Fatalities," PRWeb, May 23, 2012.
699. National Highway Traffic Safety Administration, *Blueprint for Ending Distracted Driving* (Washington, D.C.: U.S. Department of Transportation, National Highway Traffic Safety Administration, 2012). DOT HS 811 629.
700. Ibid.

701. www.forbes.com/sites/sap/2012/09/18/it-is-time-for-a-parental-control-no-texting-while-driving-phone.
702. Remarks delivered by David Strickland at the Texas Traffic Safety Conference in San Antonio, June 5, 2012.
703. www.usatoday.com/story/news/nation/2013/06/25/teen-drivers-speeding/2443459.
704. www.alcoholalert.com/drinking-and-driving.html.
705. Ibid.
706. Ibid.
707. Ibid.
708. www.businessinsider.com/worst-us-drivers-are-in-washington-dc-2013-8.
709. Ibid.
710. http://sleepfoundation.org/sleep-topics/drowsy-driving.
711. Ibid.
712. http://sleepfoundation.org/sites/default/files/Drowsy%20Driving-Key%20 Messages%20and%20Talking%20Points.pdf.
713. Ibid.
714. www.redorbit.com/news/science/1112527235/turn-signal-neglect-a-continuing-problem-in-the-us.
715. Ibid.
716. Ibid.
717. http://mentalfloss.com/article/26053/6-worst-car-accidents-recent-us-history.
718. Ibid.
719. www.nytimes.com/1990/12/12/us/15-killed-and-over-50-hurt-in-fog-as-75-vehicles-crash-in-tennessee.html.
720. Ibid.
721. http://mentalfloss.com/article/26053/6-worst-car-accidents-recent-us-history.
722. Ibid.
723. http://mentalfloss.com/article/26053/6-worst-car-accidents-recent-us-history; www.fhwa.dot.gov/publications/publicroads/01mayjun /worstcrash.cfm.
724. www.cbsnews.com/8301-505145_162-40543656/men-vs-women-who-are-safer-drivers.
725. http://usatoday30.usatoday.com/news/nation/2007-05-02-older-drivers-usat1a_N.htm.
726. Ibid.
727. Ibid.
728. Ibid.
729. www.cbsnews.com/news/89-year-old-found-guilty-of-manslaughter.
730. Ibid.
731. www.nhtsa.gov/people/injury/aggressive/aggproplanner/page05.htm.
732. Ibid.
733. www.chron.com/news/houston-texas/article/Hundreds-of-accidents-blamed-on-Houston-road-rage-3721059.php.
734. http://abclocal.go.com/wabc/story?section=news/local/new_ york&id=9267511.

735. http://news.drive.com.au/drive/motor-news/road-rage-causes-many-deaths-survey-20100804-117so.html.
736. Ibid.
737. Ibid.
738. www.cleveland.com/open/index.ssf/2013/04/ohio_must_pay_33_million_for_f.html.
739. www.nytimes.com/1991/12/01/us/scenes-of-disaster-in-pileup-that-killed-17-in-california.html.
740. www.fhwa.dot.gov/publications/publicroads/02sep/06.cfm.
741. Ibid.
742. Ibid.

21. THE 1970S, MAN

743. http://entertainment.lilithezine.com/Stephen-King.html.
744. Jon Dietz, "On-Air Shot Kills TV Personality," *Sarasota Herald-Tribune*, July 16, 1974.
745. Ibid.
746. www.howstuffworks.com/ied.htm.
747. http://history.howstuffworks.com/history-vs-myth/kent-state2.htm.
748. www.theatlantic.com/politics/archive/2011/11/i-am-not-a-kook-richard-nixons-bizarre-visit-to-the-lincoln-memorial/248443.
749. http://history.howstuffworks.com/history-vs-myth/kent-state1.htm.
750. http://content.time.com/time/magazine/article/0,9171,35056,00.html.
751. www.businessweek.com/magazine/the-nixon-shock-08042011.html.
752. http://cityroom.blogs.nytimes.com/2007/07/09/remembering-the-77-blackout/?_php=true&_type=blogs&_r=0.
753. Ibid.
754. http://sportsillustrated.cnn.com/si_online/news/2002/08/20/main.
755. Ibid.
756. Ibid.
757. www.nrc.gov/reading-rm/doc-collections/fact-sheets/3mile-isle.html.
758. www.history.com/topics/three-mile-island.
759. Ibid.
760. www.pbs.org/wgbh/americanexperience/features/general-article/carter-hostage-crisis.
761. www.history.com/topics/iran-hostage-crisis.
762. www.pbs.org/wgbh/americanexperience/features/general-article/carter-hostage-crisis.
763. www.pbs.org/wgbh/amex/vietnam/trenches/my_lai.html.
764. www.history.com/topics/my-lai-massacre.
765. www.pbs.org/wgbh/amex/vietnam/trenches/my_lai.html.
766. www.history.com/topics/my-lai-massacre.
767. www.crimelibrary.com/terrorists_spies/terrorists/hearst/1.html.
768. Ibid.
769. www.history.com/this-day-in-history/the-symbionese-liberation-army-abducts-patty-hearst.
770. Ibid.
771. Ibid.

772. www.huffingtonpost.com/2012/11/28/harvey-milk-george-moscone_n_2206107.html.
773. Ibid.
774. www.history.com/this-day-in-history/san-francisco-leaders-george-moscone-and-harvey-milk-are-murdered.
775. Ibid.
776. Ibid.

22. THE 1980S—OMIGOD!

777. www.nbcnews.com/id/3078062/ns/technology_and_science-space#.UrOUNI1RbPM.
778. www.nbcnews.com/id/11031097/ns/technology_and_science-space/t/myths-about-challenger-shuttle-disaster/#.UslpTvZRbPM.
779. http://variety.com/2006/scene/awards/spinney-cycle-1117939890.
780. www.denverpost.com/ci_22041966/remembering-michael-jackson-thriller-turns-30.
781. http://entertainment.time.com/2013/07/29/michael-jackson-and-freddie-mercury-three-duets-coming-out-this-fall.
782. www.nytimes.com/1989/04/19/us/new-twist-on-crack-in-florida.html.
783. www.dailymail.co.uk/news/article-1365456/Rawhide-shot-The-Secret-Service-tapes-Ronald-Reagan-assassination-attempt-revealed-time.html.
784. Ibid.
785. www.huffingtonpost.com/2010/12/08/john-lennon-death-mnf_n_793710.html.
786. www.nytimes.com/1988/05/16/us/hemophilia-and-aids-silent-suffering.html?.
787. http://news.bbc.co.uk/2/hi/europe/8347753.stm.
788. www.history.com/news/6-things-you-may-not-know-about-the-vietnam-veterans-memorial.
789. Ibid.
790. www.livescience.com/39961-chernobyl.html.
791. Ibid.
792. www.nrc.gov/reading-rm/doc-collections/fact-sheets/chernobyl-bg.html.
793. Ibid.
794. Ibid.
795. www.livescience.com/27553-mount-st-helens-eruption.html.
796. www.wired.com/thisdayintech/2009/12/dayintech_1202jarvikheart.
797. www.npr.org/news/graphics/2008/june/bill_gates/gates_timeline_04.html.
798. http://adventure.howstuffworks.com/outdoor-activities/urban-sports/buildering2.htm.

23. ERECTILE DYSFUNCTION MEDICATION

799. www.sciencedaily.com/releases/2010/09/100927155318.htm.
800. www.washingtonpost.com/wp-dyn/content/article/2008/12/25/AR2008122500931.html.
801. www.cnbc.com/id/44759526.

802. www.forbes.com/sites/melaniehaiken/2013/09/12/buying-viagra-online-its-very-likely-fake-and-possibly-dangerous-new-data-say.
803. Ibid.
804. Ibid.
805. Ibid.
806. www.viagra.com/safety-information.aspx.
807. www.telegraph.co.uk/news/uknews/law-and-order/4925836/Drug-dealers-switching-from-cocaine-to-fake-Viagra.html.
808. http://nfl.si.com/2012/11/28/brandon-marshall-ive-heard-of-players-using-viagra-to-get-an-edge.
809. www.huffingtonpost.com/2013/09/23/gentil-ramirez-penis-surgery-amputated-viagra_n_3975407.html.
810. www.foxnews.com/story/2009/02/26/man-28-dies-after-guzzling-viagra-during-12-hour-romp.
811. www.nbcnews.com/health/too-much-good-thing-4-hour-erection-1C9926694.
812. www.britannica.com/EBchecked/topic/475721/Priapus.
813. www.webmd.com/erectile-dysfunction/guide/erectile-dysfunction-priapism.
814. Ibid.
815. http://abcnews.go.com/blogs/health/2012/05/01/man-blames-bmw-for-long-lasting-erection.
816. www.huffingtonpost.com/2012/08/29/spider-venom-viagra-brazilian-wandering_n_1840381.html.

24. DRINKS THAT AREN'T GOOD FOR YOU

817. www.prevention.com/food/healthy-eating-tips/diet-soda-bad-you.
818. Ibid.
819. www.hungryforchange.tv/article/are-diet-sodas-making-us-fat.
820. Ibid.
821. www.today.com/health/diet-soda-doing-these-7-awful-things-your-body-1C6558748.
822. www.prevention.com/food/healthy-eating-tips/diet-soda-bad-you; http://www.health.com/health/gallery/0,20739512,00.html.
823. www.today.com/health/diet-soda-doing-these-7-awful-things-your-body-1C6558748.
824. www.cbsnews.com/8301-504763_162-20075358-10391704/new-study-is-wake-up-call-for-diet-soda-drinkers; www.hungryforchange.tv/article/are-diet-sodas-making-us-fat.
825. http://www.health.com/health/gallery/0,20739512,00.html.
826. www.hungryforchange.tv/article/are-diet-sodas-making-us-fat.
827. Ibid.
828. http://www.health.com/health/gallery/0,20739512,00.html.
829. www.hungryforchange.tv/article/are-diet-sodas-making-us-fat.
830. www.today.com/health/diet-soda-doing-these-7-awful-things-your-body-1C6558748.
831. Ibid.

832. www.prevention.com/food/healthy-eating-tips/diet-soda-bad-you.
833. Ibid.
834. http://www.health.com/health/gallery/0,20739512,00.html.
835. www.prevention.com/food/healthy-eating-tips/diet-soda-bad-you.
836. www.today.com/health/diet-soda-doing-these-7-awful-things-your-body-1C6558748.
837. www.drweil.com/drw/u/QAA400466/Is-Bottled-Flavored-Green-Tea-Bad.html.
838. well.blogs.nytimes.com/2013/05/23/whats-in-your-green-tea/?_r=0.
839. Ibid.
840. https://www.consumerlab.com/reviews/Green_Tea_Review_Supplements_and_Bottled/Green_Tea/.
841. Ibid.
842. http://well.blogs.nytimes.com/2013/05/23/whats-in-your-green-tea/?_r=0.
843. http://naturallysavvy.com/eat/whats-really-in-your-cup-of-green-tea.
844. www.nytimes.com/2013/01/12/business/more-emergency-room-visits-linked-to-energy-drinks-report-says.html?_r=0.
845. www.webmd.com/food-recipes/news/20080924/energy-drinks-hazardous-to-your-health.
846. Ibid.
847. http://brown.edu/Student_Services/Health_Services/Health_Education/alcohol,_tobacco,_&_other_drugs/energy_drinks.php.
848. www.globalhealingcenter.com/natural-health/health-dangers-of-energy-drinks.
849. www.nlm.nih.gov/medlineplus/ency/article/002579.htm.
850. www.medicalnewstoday.com/articles/255078.php.
851. www.nytimes.com/2013/01/12/business/more-emergency-room-visits-linked-to-energy-drinks-report-says.html?_r=0.
852. www.medicalnewstoday.com/articles/255078.php.
853. www.nytimes.com/2013/01/12/business/more-emergency-room-visits-linked-to-energy-drinks-report-says.html?_r=0.
854. http://brown.edu/Student_Services/Health_Services/Health_Education/alcohol,_tobacco,_&_other_drugs/energy_drinks.php.
855. Ibid.
856. www.webmd.com/food-recipes/news/20080924/energy-drinks-hazardous-to-your-health.
857. www.cdc.gov/alcohol/fact-sheets/cab.htm.
858. Ibid.
859. http://brown.edu/Student_Services/Health_Services/Health_Education/alcohol,_tobacco,_&_other_drugs/energy_drinks.php.
860. Ibid.
861. www.webmd.com/food-recipes/news/20080924/energy-drinks-hazardous-to-your-health.
862. www.ncbi.nlm.nih.gov/pubmed/23315697.
863. www.globalhealingcenter.com/natural-health/health-dangers-of-energy-drinks.
864. Ibid.
865. Ibid.

866. www.mandatory.com/2013/07/03/10-of-the-freakiest-freak-accidents-ever.

867. www.newser.com/story/101564/segway-accident-kills-segway-co-owner.html.

868. http://abcnews.go.com/US/story?id=92745&page=1.

869. www.mandatory.com/2013/07/03/10-of-the-freakiest-freak-accidents-ever/.

870. www.nytimes.com/1995/01/15/us/campus-s-killer-moose-destroyed-in-alaska.html.

871. www.foxnews.com/us/2013/08/18/year-old-utah-girl-dies-in-freak-trampoline-accident.

872. www.mandatory.com/2013/07/03/10-of-the-freakiest-freak-accidents-ever.

873. www.telegraph.co.uk/news/uknews/7982808/Former-member-of-ELO-killed-by-hay-bale-while-driving.html.

874. www.mandatory.com/2013/07/03/10-of-the-freakiest-freak-accidents-ever.

875. www.telegraph.co.uk/news/picturegalleries/celebritynews/7984944/Mike-Edwards-hay-bale-death-celebrities-in-freak-killings.html.

876. http://news.bbc.co.uk/2/hi/africa/203137.stm.

877. www.dailymail.co.uk/news/article-2130244/Killer-swan-attacks-caretaker-Anthony-Hensley-kayak-Death-ruled-drowning.html.

878. www.mandatory.com/2013/07/03/10-of-the-freakiest-freak-accidents-ever.

879. www.theguardian.com/world/2012/aug/27/javelin-accident-kills-german?newsfeed=true.

880. http://gawker.com/5924191/four+year+old-boy-crushed-by-falling-tombstone.

881. www.mandatory.com/2013/07/03/10-of-the-freakiest-freak-accidents-ever.

882. Ibid.

883. Ibid.

884. www.huffingtonpost.com/2013/03/07/coach-dies-in-freak-accident-rio-linda-marion-adams_n_2829869.html.

885. www.huffingtonpost.com/2011/12/15/repairman-jason-jordan-ch_n_1151423.html.

886. Ibid.

887. http://blogs.wsj.com/metropolis/2013/09/05/remote-control-helicopter-kills-man-in-brooklyn.

888. www.newser.com/story/119194/spanish-cyclist-xavier-tondo-dies-in-freak-garage-accident.html.

889. www.mandatory.com/2013/07/03/10-of-the-freakiest-freak-accidents-ever.

890. www.nhregister.com/general-news/20110413/a-true-tragedy-yale-student-asphyxiated-in-lathe-accident-at-chemistry-lab-medical-examiner-rules?viewmode=fullstory.

891. http://abcnews.go.com/US/bride-paralyzed-freak-bachelorette-party-accident/story?id=12163284.
892. www.newser.com/story/60069/mike-tysons-daughter-accidentally-strangled.html.
893. www.newser.com/story/22085/stingray-kills-boater-off-fla-keys.html.
894. www.ndtv.com/article/india/indian-origin-teenager-killed-in-us-in-freak-accident-416348.
895. www.mandatory.com/2013/07/03/10-of-the-freakiest-freak-accidents-ever.
896. www.cbsnews.com/8301-505263_162-57592421/parasailing-company-issues-statement-after-freak-accident-leaves-teen-girls-in-critical-condition.
897. http://fox4kc.com/2013/03/22/boy-dies-after-being-hit-by-display-board-at-ala-airport.
898. www.theblaze.com/stories/2013/04/02/new-footage-of-fla-sinkhole-that-swallowed-and-killed-a-man-released.
899. http://quemas.mamaslatinas.com/in_the_news/117640/little_girl_suffocates_to_death.
900. www.lex18.com/news/campbellsville-university-employee-killed-in-freak-accident.
901. http://articles.orlandosentinel.com/2012-08-15/news/os-lawnmower-killed-traffic-crash-20120815_1_freak-accident-yucatan-drive-troopers.
902. http://articles.baltimoresun.com/1995-10-24/news/1995297053_1_vacuum-cleaner-circuit-city-freak-accident.
903. www.sfgate.com/bayarea/article/Driver-killed-on-I-580-in-freak-accident-4539601.php.
904. www.smh.com.au/nsw/fathers-death-a-freak-accident-20120629-2181z.html.
905. www.freepresshouston.com/featured/mondo-houston-freak-accidents.
906. Ibid.
907. Ibid.
908. www.cbsnews.com/8301-504083_162-57590923-504083/miguel-martinez-14-dies-after-apparent-bizarre-accident-on-texas-tech-campus.
909. http://gothamist.com/2012/09/02/before_fatal_freak_party_bus_accide.php.
910. www.ynaija.com/freak-accident-man-crushed-to-death-by-sanitation-truck-after-falling-asleep-in-trash-bin.
911. www.cbc.ca/news/canada/toronto/pasta-company-fined-120k-in-fatal-freak-accident-1.1378070.

26. THINGS THAT STINK AND THEN KILL YOU

912. www.washingtonpost.com/wp-dyn/content/article/2005/10/05/AR2005100500908.html.
913. Ibid.
914. www.infoplease.com/encyclopedia/science/mercaptan.html.
915. http://electrical.about.com/od/electricaldevices/qt/defectiveswitch.htm.
916. www.washingtonpost.com/wp-dyn/content/article/2005/10/05/AR2005100500908.html.

917. Ibid.
918. www.forensicconstructionexpert.com/basement_air.html.
919. www.hgtvremodels.com/interiors/choosing-eco-friendly-carpet/index .html.
920. www.sixwise.com/newsletters/05/03/22/the-toxic-dangers-of-carpetingare-the-carpets-in-your-home-or-office-a-health-hazard.htm.
921. Ibid.
922. Ibid.
923. www.nontoxic.com/purewoolcarpets/whattoavoid.html.
924. www.dailymail.co.uk/health/article-1327910/Paint-fumes-trigger-asthma-cancer-Hidden-dangers-decorating.html.
925. Ibid.
926. Ibid.
927. www.iarc.fr/en/media-centre/pr/2007/pr180.html.
928. http://onlinelibrary.wiley.com/doi/10.1002/ajim.4700110403/abstract.
929. http://news.bbc.co.uk/2/hi/health/7416405.stm.
930. http://pets.webmd.com/dogs/guide/bad-breath-dogs.
931. Ibid.
932. Ibid.
933. www.agf.gov.bc.ca/pesticides/b_2.htm.
934. http://healthland.time.com/2013/04/18/ammonia-exposure.
935. www.extension.purdue.edu/extmedia/ID/cafo/ID-361-W.pdf.
936. Ibid.
937. www.cancer.org/cancer/cancercauses/othercarcinogens/pollution/diesel-exhaust.
938. Ibid.
939. Ibid.
940. www.health.ny.gov/environmental/outdoors/air/landfill_gas.htm.
941. Ibid.
942. Francesca Gould, *Why You Shouldn't Eat Your Boogers and Other Useless Information about Your Body* (Tarcher/Penguin, 2007).
943. www.lifescript.com/health/centers/diabetes/articles/bad_body_odor_ what_it_says_about_your_health.aspx.
944. www.webmd.com/skin-problems-and-treatments/guide/candidiasis-yeast-infection.
945. Ibid.
946. www.webmd.com/a-to-z-guides/urinary-tract-infections-in-teens-and-adults-topic-overview.
947. www.lifescript.com/health/centers/diabetes/articles/bad_body_odor_ what_it_says_about_your_health.aspx.
948. www.livestrong.com/article/280574-changes-in-body-odor-health.
949. Ibid.
950. www.nlm.nih.gov/medlineplus/ency/article/007259.htm.
951. www.mayoclinic.org/diseases-conditions/acromegaly/basics/definition /con-20019216.
952. Ibid.
953. http://animal.discovery.com/insects/stinkbug-info.htm.
954. www.dentalfearcentral.org/fears/dental-environment.

955. http://nursinglink.monster.com/benefits/articles/21609-10-funky-hospital-smells?page=3.
956. www.armystudyguide.com/content/Prep_For_Basic_Training/basic_training_prep_articles/to-the-gas-chambers.shtml.
957. http://healthyliving.msn.com/health-wellness/surprising-things-that-make-you-stink.
958. Ibid.
959. Ibid.
960. Ibid.
961. Ibid.

27. DOOMSDAY SCENARIOS

962. www.wired.com/wiredscience/2012/01/scientific-doomsday-scenarios/?pid=2881.
963. http://news.nationalgeographic.com/news/2011/01/110119-yellowstone-park-supervolcano-eruption-magma-science.
964. Ibid.
965. www.popularmechanics.com/science/environment/natural-disasters/12-ways-the-world-could-really-end-in-2012.
966. www.bbc.co.uk/sn/tvradio/programmes/supervolcano/article.shtml.
967. Ibid.
968. www.popularmechanics.com/science/environment/natural-disasters/12-ways-the-world-could-really-end-in-2012.
969. www.wired.com/wiredscience/2012/01/scientific-doomsday-scenarios/?pid=2881.
970. Ibid.
971. http://news.nationalgeographic.com/news/2013/13/130214-biggest-asteroid-impacts-meteorites-space-2012da14/?rptregcta=reg_free_np&rptregcampaign=20131016_rw_membership_r1p_us_dr_w#finished.
972. www.wired.com/wiredscience/2012/01/scientific-doomsday-scenarios/?pid=2881.
973. http://neo.jpl.nasa.gov.
974. http://neo.jpl.nasa.gov/apophis.
975. www.wired.com/wiredscience/2012/01/scientific-doomsday-scenarios/?pid=2881.
976. Ibid.
977. http://imagine.gsfc.nasa.gov/docs/science/know_l2/supernovae.html.
978. www.nasa.gov/centers/goddard/news/topstory/2003/0108supernova.html.
979. www.wired.com/wiredscience/2012/01/scientific-doomsday-scenarios/?pid=2881.
980. www.popularmechanics.com/science/environment/natural-disasters/12-ways-the-world-could-really-end-in-2012/.
981. www.livescience.com/14173-doomsday-scenarios-apocalypse-2012.html.
982. www.wired.com/wiredscience/2012/01/scientific-doomsday-scenarios.
983. http://www.kansascity.com/2014/02/15/4826370/could-a-giant-sunburst-unplug.html.

984. www.wired.com/wiredscience/2012/01/scientific-doomsday-scenarios.
985. http://news.nationalgeographic.com/news/2008/01/080110-black-holes
.html; http://www.cracked.com/article_19117_7-horrible-ways-universe-
can-destroy-us-without-warning.html.
986. http://showcase.netins.net/web/d503/Some%20fear%20debut%20of%20
powerful%20atom-smasher%20-%20CNN_com.htm.
987. www.trutv.com/conspiracy/phenomena/doomsday-scenarios/gallery
.html?curPhoto=1.
988. Ibid.
989. http://discovermagazine.com/2010/oct/30-ways-the-world-could-end#
.UhrDDZKsiSo.
990. http://dsc.discovery.com/tv-shows/curiosity/topics/20-ways-world-might-
end.htm.
991. Ibid.
992. www.popularmechanics.com/science/environment/natural-disasters/12-
ways-the-world-could-really-end-in-2012/.
993. www.livescience.com/36999-top-scientists-world-enders.html.
994. www.popularmechanics.com/science/environment/natural-disasters/12-
ways-the-world-could-really-end-in-2012/.
995. Ibid.
996. http://computer.howstuffworks.com/moores-law.htm.
997. www.popularmechanics.com/science/environment/natural-disasters/12-
ways-the-world-could-really-end-in-2012/.
998. http://discovermagazine.com/2000/oct/featworld#.Uhq8zpKsiSp; www
.popularmechanics.com/science/environment/natural-disasters/12-ways-
the-world-could-really-end-in-2012.
999. http://discovermagazine.com/2000/oct/featworld#.Uhq8zpKsiSp; www
.popularmechanics.com/science/environment/natural-disasters/12-ways-
the-world-could-really-end-in-2012.
1000. www.trutv.com/conspiracy/phenomena/doomsday-scenarios/gallery
.html?curPhoto=1.
1001. www.dailymail.co.uk/news/article-505009/September-26th-1983-The-day-
world-died.html.
1002. www.popularmechanics.com/science/environment/natural-disasters/12-
ways-the-world-could-really-end-in-2012/.
1003. Ibid.
1004. www.livescience.com/36999-top-scientists-world-enders.html.

ACKNOWLEDGMENTS

I AM GRATEFUL for the many people who helped bring this book to life: Holly Schmidt, Allan Penn, Becky Thomas, and Monica Sweeney at Hollan Publishing; Meg Leder and John Duff at Perigee Books; my researcher, Connie Biltz; Cyndi Culpepper, Rachael Pavlik, Amy Carey, Kip Sears, and Jillian Nord; and my wife and daughter.

ABOUT THE AUTHOR

CARY McNEAL has written four books, including the bestselling *1,001 Facts That Will Scare the S#*t Out of You*, *Crap I Bought on eBay*, and *Scared Sh*tless*.

Visit him online at
listoftheday.net and facebook.com/ScaredShtless.